Yes, You Can...

Raise Financially Aware Kids

Yes, You Can...
Raise Financially Aware Kids

CREATED BY JACK JONATHAN

WITH

DEBORAH SHOUSE

NANCY O'NEILL

DR. SHEELAGH MANHEIM

SAM GOLLER

ALEXIS PRESTON

ILLUSTRATED BY

PAUL COKER, JR.

Discover the good life!™

STOWERS INNOVATIONS
INC
An American Century Investments Company

Yes, You Can… Raise Financially Aware Kids
First Edition
© 2002, 2006, 2008, 2010 by Stowers Innovations, Inc.
For information write:
Yes, You Can…
4500 Main Street, Kansas City, Missouri 64111-7709.

ISBN 13: 978-0-9629788-8-3: $19.95
Library of Congress Card Number: 2002109354

When I was growing up, my parents did not want me to work for money. They wanted me to play, concentrate on my studies, learn music and not be distracted by worrying about earning money.

Even though the path I followed led me to great wealth, I was extremely fortunate to have learned the practical facts about money on my own, because I was not made aware of any of the important information at home or while in school.

As I look back on my childhood, I realize my parents did teach me a great deal about how to succeed and achieve my goals. They convinced me, by their examples and teachings, that if I was absolutely determined to do my very best, I could succeed at anything ... including achieving financial independence.

It is important that your children learn what they can do with money early in life so they will apply the lessons learned at home as they face the real world in future years.

Like an acorn, every child holds great potential, needing only time, nourishment and the right place to grow. The information in this book will help you create the groundwork that will nurture your children and make them aware of the many financial principles that will affect their future.

James E. Stowers

Founder, American Century Investments
Co-Founder, Stowers Institute for Medical Research
Author of *Yes, You Can... Achieve Financial Independence*
and *The Best is Yet to Be*

Whive working with James E. Stowers on the development of *Yes, You Can… Achieve Financial Independence*, the idea came to me for a book written for parents to help their children become financially aware. Although *Yes, You Can* is designed to help people reach financial independence, I feel there is also a need to help children learn the value of a dollar. As Mr. Stowers stated in his first book, "Time is money, but money is not nearly as valuable without time." So what better time is there to begin preparing for financial independence than in childhood? And what better teacher is there for your children than you, their parent?

Ten years after *Yes, You Can… Achieve Financial Independence* was first published, a team of enthusiastic contributors and I began gathering research to create *Yes, You Can… Raise Financially Aware Kids.* Interviews and focus groups were held, while books, Web sites, magazine and newspaper articles were collected and reviewed to provide this comprehensive tool to help you raise financially aware children.

Special recognition goes to Deborah Shouse, whose talent in organization and writing skills were able to reflect my earliest vision for this book. My thanks go to Nancy O'Neill, Sam Goller and Dr. Sheelagh Manheim for their tireless editing and content contributions, and to Alexis Preston, whose creative development of the "Ability" sections helped provide practical learning experiences for principles throughout the book. Credit also goes to Annette Paxton for pulling together and organizing the research material.

My appreciation and admiration goes to Paul Coker, Jr. His inspired illustrations bring life and humor to our words, while his editing insights helped to create a clear, concise message. Book designer Frank Addington found creative solutions to pull words and illustrations together to bring this project to fruition.

I also want to acknowledge our Editorial Board, which included: Mindy Ball, Carol Hillboldt, Holly Howe, Beth Kaplan, Richard Lee, Jennifer O'Neill and Michael Stahl. Their enthusiastic contributions, creativity and experiences provided valuable feedback and original "Ability" ideas.

Finally, I want to thank Jim Stowers. In addition to being my toughest critic, Jim is also a source of inspiration. His philosophies regarding life and money have made a lasting impression on me and are the basis for many of the ideas in this book.

Jack Jonathan

You are the head of a small consumer empire. From age two onward your children become advertising targets. You are one of their only shields. You are your children's best link to financial health. This Foreword introduces you as a prime financial resource and explains the concept of the book.

- **Ready, Aim!**
- **Money Matters**
- **Yes, You Can! And It's Easy**
- **Money Makes the World Go and Grow**

The Story and History of Money: The Message is in the Medium

Money has experienced many changes. This chapter is dotted with historical tidbits and gives you a quick and flavorful biography of money's evolution as a medium of exchange. Through this chapter, you and your children will be exploring:

- **Barter Power**
- **What Is Money and How Did It Evolve?**
- **Banks and the Federal Reserve**
- **The Future of Money**

Chapter 2

Money Values

This chapter further explains your role as **CFP (Chief Financial Parent)** and guides you into exploring your own financial history. The more you understand your own money "heritage," the better you're able to be a financial role model for your children. This chapter invites you to explore and define the role of money in your life.

- Become a Chief Financial Parent
- Money Talks – And You Listened
- Money Values
- Your Starring Role as a Money Model
- Bringing Your Values to Life
- Who Needs It? Who Wants It?
- Talk is Valuable and a Great Investment

Chapter 3

The Allowance Experience

An allowance is an inexpensive way to give your children a lesson in money management.

This chapter introduces you to two steps in the allowance experience:

FIRST STEP: Preparing to Give an Allowance
- Decide on Your Allowance Philosophy
- Noticing Allowance Readiness
- Determining How Much and How Often
- Setting the Allowance Rules

SECOND STEP: Evaluating Allowances
- Being There for Your Children
- Raising Allowances
- Handling Issues and Solving Problems
- Performing an Allowance Review

Chapter 4 89

Money Ins and Outs: Achieving Your Financial Goals

Talking about spending and budgeting gives you a chance to show your children how to express their values in the ways they earn, save and spend money. This chapter discusses:

- **Involving Your Children in the Finances of Everyday Life**
- **Developing Your Children's Budget**
- **Home-Based Work and Earning Opportunities**
- **Working for Others**
- **Checkbooks and Balances**
- **Credit Cards and Beyond**

Chapter 5 129

Putting Your Money to Work

You and your children may dream of earning money while you sleep. However, before this can happen, your children need to set aside some money to invest. The first step in the investment process is understanding how time and money work together.

- **Why Save Money?**
- **The Shrinking Dollar**
- **How Time and Money Work Together**
- **Banking on Savings**
- **Money Markets, CDs and Other Savings Instruments**

Chapter 6 155

Growing Money Right: Investing

Once your children have accumulated some money in a savings account, they may want to consider investing to help it grow over time. This chapter explores the benefits and risks of different investment options.

- **The Investing Decision**
- **Owning Property by Collecting**
- **Your Children and the Stock Market**
- **Mutual Funds Offer a Diverse Investment**
- **Buying and Selling**
- **Investment Attributes Chart**

Chapter 7 179

Smart Spending: Becoming a Wise Consumer

Part of being financially aware is learning how to be a wise consumer. This chapter invites your children to understand their power in the marketplace and to realize the kind of power the market has over them. You'll also share ways to make smart purchases and talk about:

- **Understanding the Purchase Decision**
- **Comparison Shopping**
- **How and When to Negotiate**
- **Knowing Your Consumer Rights**
- **Keeping an Eye on On-Line Shopping**
- **Running on Empty**

Chapter 8

Donations and Volunteering

The ideal philanthropy matches your children's talents, interests and values with a need. Kids love to feel like they are helping and the ideal giving experience is exciting and energizing to your children. This chapter discusses:

- **Exploring Your Children's Giving Style**
- **Finding Causes Your Children Like**
- **Discovering Volunteer Opportunities**
- **Using Family Funds for Giving**
- **Giving to Family and Friends**
- **Feeling Thankful**

Chapter 9

Smart Learning: How to Keep Getting the Financial Information You Need

As a devoted CFP, you've given your children a great beginning for their financial future. This chapter invites you to give them some tools they can take with them wherever they go. You'll discuss:

- **Putting Money in Perspective**
- **Investing in Learning**
- **Asking for Help: Finding Experts and Mentors**
- **Letting Them Learn**

Additional Resources

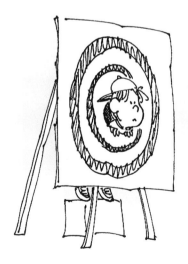

Every day your children are targets.

Ready, Aim!

Every day your children are targets. Thousands of marketers are aiming right at your kids and their aim often hits the mark. Before your children turn five years old, they have been hit by at least 30,000 advertisements. These ads are aimed at turning your vulnerable, impressionable, curious children into insatiable consumers.

As consumers, your children are part of a growing market that directly influenced $188 billion and indirectly influenced $300 billion more of parental spending. Children contributed $25 billion of their own money to the mix. That's why it's important that you talk to your children and prepare them to be smart consumers.

Money Matters

Most schools do not include financial education as part of their curriculum. A recent survey of high school students revealed that about 88% of what they know about finances, they learned from their parents. This wasn't through formal teaching and conversations; but through observing how their parents earned, spent and talked about money.

The moment you became a parent, you became your children's **CFP – Chief Financial Parent.** You are your children's main resource, guide and teacher in financial education and responsibility.

As CFPs, many of us may not feel prepared to be our children's major source of financial information. Yet, we want our children to have strong values, to be financially astute, and to be "successful" in ways that include living a balanced life, choosing work they like, earning a good living, and being generous and compassionate.

Children are quick to pick up on clues. Just seeing or knowing that you bought this book and intend to work with them is a message that you think financial education is important.

Many of us may not feel prepared to be our children's major source of financial information.

Yes, You Can! And It's Easy

Consider these questions:

- **Do you want your children to learn financial responsibility?**
- **Do you want your children's future quality of life to be as good as or better than yours?**
- **Do you want your children to have the tools they need to make sound financial decisions?**
- **Do you need help guiding your children in the process of becoming financially aware?**
- **Do your children respond to fun and interactive activities when learning lifelong lessons?**

Do you want your children to enjoy a quality of life as good as or better than you have?

If you answered "yes" to one or more of these questions, you'll find this book a valuable resource in guiding your children toward good financial habits and values.

We've taken the principles of child development you've read about in parenting books and applied them to the basic financial concepts you want your children to experience. **Money, budgeting, saving, and gift giving mean different things at each of your children's developmental phases.** We give you the basic information you need to guide your children's learning. Then we offer age-appropriate activities, to fit your children's level of development, from preschool through high school.

The learning activities are listed under the **Ability** sections found at the back of each chapter. The fun and interactive projects in each **Ability** section are designed to enrich your children's financial skills while illustrating the principles and lessons outlined in each chapter. The **Ability** sections are divided into the following four categories:

Preschool
3 to 5 years old

Elementary School
6 to 11 years old

Middle School
12 to 14 years old

High School
15 to 18 years old

Each age group may not be represented in each **Ability** section. For instance, because the information discussed in Chapter 1: The Story and History of Money has most likely been learned at an early age, few activities for the High School level have been included. Regardless of your children's ages, if you feel your kids would benefit from any of the activities listed under any age level, please give them a try!

*To have the most positive impact, look for opportunities to talk about finances or to initiate **Ability** activities whenever you and your children are together. Your best opportunities may occur when you're driving to and from school, or while wheeling around the grocery store.*

In addition to the **Ability** sections, you'll find activities throughout the chapters designed to help you prepare for your role in guiding your children's financial future. These activities will help you understand your beliefs about money and the financial concepts being discussed.

We have also provided note space to write down goals you may have for your children and to record your successes, challenges and ideas. As your children grow, you can revisit this book, review your thoughts and see where time and knowledge have taken your family financially.

Money Makes the World Go and Grow

Being financially responsible means different things to different families. This book gives you ideas and options that will help you explore what financial responsibility means to you and to your children. You'll be urged to make financial talk a part of your regular conversations and to encourage your children to mature into their own financial personality with their own financial dreams and goals.

You are the ideal teacher for your children. You know what sparks their interests. By using this book, you turn some of the time you're already spending with your children into a fun learning experience – one that will last them a lifetime.

Most kids learn about finances by observing their parents.

THE STORY AND HISTORY OF MONEY:
The Message is in the Medium

Our ancestors ate the food they grew or caught and
slept in whatever shelter they could easily find.

oney has experienced many changes. This chapter is dotted with historical tidbits and gives you a quick and flavorful biography of money's evolution as a medium of exchange. By sharing money histories and stories with your kids, you help them put money into perspective and show them how it has been used. Here are the topics you'll be exploring:

- **BARTER POWER introduces bartering as a natural part of your children's lives and possibly of your own.**

- **WHAT IS MONEY AND HOW DID IT EVOLVE? gives you a quick history of the evolution of money.**

- **BANKS AND THE FEDERAL RESERVE. Imagine going to your bank and learning they are temporarily out of cash! That's where the Federal Reserve comes in – regulating money and the money supply.**

- **THE FUTURE OF MONEY invites you to imagine money in the late 21st century.**

Barter Power

These days, many of us dream of a simpler life. It's tempting to think that life was better when long ago, in the BCC (Before Credit Cards) era, no one carried a wallet, hoarded gold coins, or stuffed money into mattresses for those rainy days. It was certainly different – our ancestors ate the food they grew or caught and slept in whatever shelter they could easily find. But things soon changed.

People became aware of their own unique skills and qualities. One person was a great storyteller and another a great farmer. One was a wonderful hunter and another a skilled canoe maker. How could the canoe maker get some of the hunter's meat? And how could the hunter get some of the farmer's vegetables, without getting into a big stew about it?

Tomatoes might be valuable... but only if they are not held too long.

Our ancestors were motivated, as we are, by the desire to acquire something beyond what they could make, grow or earn. So they began to trade articles and services without using money. This is called bartering. Bartering worked well for thousands of years, even though it was sometimes cumbersome and often inconvenient.

You wouldn't go shopping without your fish...

- First, you had to find someone who wanted what you had. A farmer who wanted to trade corn for a mule had to find a mule owner who wanted some corn.

- Then you had to agree on values. The value of things constantly changed. One day you might exchange an axe for a bushel of corn and the next day, a farmer might be willing to trade a whole cow for the axe.

- Finally, you had to be quick about it. Just as "time waits for no man," bartering holds a certain immediacy. Some things do not age well and have to be traded immediately. A beautiful, vine-ripened tomato has only so many good days before it loses value.

What Is Money and How Did It Evolve?

Money has taken many interesting forms in its long career. In the early 18th century, the Native Americans traded with "wampum" – polished beads made from seashells and strung together in belts. The settlers also traded grain, gunpowder and fish. Other cultures used large stone disks, cowry shells, copper rings or farming implements to make payments and settle debts.

Imagine checking your purse to make sure you had your block of salt, beads, stones, fish or beer before you headed off shopping.

Ideally, money is:

- **Easy to handle,**
- **Reliable, so it can serve as a predictable and constant standard of value,**
- **Universally accepted as a medium of exchange,**
- **Divisible into easily identifiable units of measurement.**

Money Lite: Money Goes Thin

Imagine going on a trip with your pockets and purses bulging with hundreds of coins. The weight of the trip could be instantly lightened by robbers, so people began leaving their money with goldsmiths and carrying a receipt instead. The receipt was an early form of traveler's check – you simply exchanged the receipt for coins with a goldsmith when you got to your destination. The receipts became so commonplace that people began paying debts with them, rather than with coins. This was the beginning of paper money.

In the mid 17th century, banks in the United States began printing paper bank notes, which were issued to people who deposited their coins in the bank. Each note stated the number of coins the person would receive from the bank.

Legal Tender: All the Money That's Fit to Print

In America, the Congress of the original 13 colonies printed paper money to finance the Revolutionary War. **During the Civil War, the government couldn't come up with enough gold and silver coins to finance the conflict, so they printed paper money.** They called these notes Legal Tender, meaning the notes had to be accepted for all private debts.

The government couldn't come up with enough gold and silver coins, so they printed up paper money.

Banks and the Federal Reserve

Independence is great, but not necessarily when it comes to regulating the money supply. Imagine going to your bank for money, only to learn that they are temporarily "out of cash!" That's what happened in the early 20th century. Small banks deposited their cash in larger banks, which in turn, sent their cash to big city banks. If dozens of farmers lined up to withdraw money, because of a dry season and a poor crop, the small bank could easily be high and dry itself, quickly running out of money. Naturally, this made people feel uneasy – and often led to money panics. These panics inspired the creation of the Federal Reserve in 1913.

The Federal Reserve (Fed) is a system of 12 regional reserve banks which manage the reserves of all nationally chartered banks. The Federal Reserve Board of Governors in Washington, D.C. supervises and administers the overall operation of this system.

The Federal Reserve performs these functions:

- **Conducts the nation's money policy,**
- **Supervises and regulates banks and protects the credit rights of the consumer,**
- **Maintains the stability of our financial system,**
- **Provides financial services to the government, public, financial institutions and foreign official institutions.**

Source: http://federalreserve.gov/

National banks must be members of the Federal Reserve System and the Federal Deposit Insurance Corporation (FDIC). When member banks require more currency, they can obtain it by drawing on their account at the Federal Reserve Banks. If they need more than is in their accounts, the banks can pledge other assets.

The Future of Money

Some kids think money grows in ATMs or comes from credit cards. Our money has become consistently "lighter," from heavy metals to paper notes. Now, with the advent of checks, credit and debit cards, and telephone or Internet bill paying, actual cash may never change hands. We depend increasingly on electronic transactions. Banking, bill paying and purchasing goods and services can all be done without leaving our homes. Our hands never need to touch paper currency or coins. Convenience and the security of not carrying money have proven to be important advantages for many people.

MONEY MATTERS

Electronic transactions are financial dealings that are made through the use of computers – without a single dollar bill changing hands.

Some kids think money grows in ATMs.

THE STORY AND HISTORY OF MONEY

Abilities

Story Time • Lunch and Learn • Let's Make a Deal

Money, Money, Money • Silly Store • Making Cents

More Than a Candy Store • Adventures of a Bill • The ATM Experience

Become an ATM

BARTER POWER

Story Time

What better way is there to spend an afternoon than to have your children curled up with you as you read them a favorite book. It makes for a relaxing time together and can also prompt great conversations.

Read ***Jack and the Beanstalk*** to your children. Be sure to point out how Jack traded or "bartered" his cow for magic beans. Discuss the following:

- Is a cow worth a few beans?

- Did Jack's mother think he had bartered wisely?

- What else could Jack have traded for the cow?

- Did his trade end up being a good one? Why?

 CFP TIP

If you are spending $5 a day to eat lunch out, you are spending more than $1,200 a year on lunches. If you brought a peanut butter sandwich from home for lunch instead, you could save about $1,000 that could then be invested.

BARTER POWER

Lunch and Learn

Sometimes, the best way for kids to learn is through their stomachs! To complete this lesson, you will need at least three hungry participants. The fun begins as they barter with each other to make their lunches. The best part is, everyone wins and gets to eat lunch!

- Gather the items needed for a lunch, i.e., bread, peanut butter, jelly, milk, chips and cookies.

- Distribute the items to each participant. Participant 1 – bread and cookies; Participant 2 – milk and peanut butter; Participant 3 – jelly and chips.

- Participants are then encouraged to barter or trade with each other in order to make their lunch.

This game can be made even more interesting by assigning roles to the participants, e.g., the baker, the milk man or the peanut butter maker.

BARTER POWER

Let's Make a Deal

Do chores sometimes pile up in your house because everyone is so busy? This exercise not only lets your family practice bartering skills, but will also help keep household chores from being left undone!

- Create a card for each chore or task that needs to be completed for the week. The tasks need to be simple enough that anyone can do them.

- Put the cards in a hat and have each family member draw until all the cards are gone.

If a family member draws a task he doesn't like or doesn't have time to do (and hopefully someone will), have them try to "make a deal" with another family member.

Chores that no one wants to do (such as "Cleaning the bathroom") may equal two other chores.

EXAMPLE: Someone draws "Wash dishes after dinner," but can't do it on Monday and Wednesday because of baseball practice. That family member might barter or trade with the person who drew "Straighten living and family rooms" for those days. If no one will trade tasks, family members can offer services or goods for others to do their chores. "I will let you wear my _____ two times if you do the dishes for me on those days."

YOUR IDEAS AND EXPERIENCES

WHAT IS MONEY AND HOW DID IT EVOLVE?

Money, Money, Money

Bigger is better, at least that's the way many of us think. The same is true for children, who sometimes think a nickel is worth more than a dime because it's bigger. Make this money drawer with your children to help them learn the value of coins.

What you will need:

- 25 pennies, 10 nickels, 10 dimes and 4 quarters

- A separating container for the money drawer, i.e., a muffin pan or an empty egg carton

- Tags or stickers to label the compartments or containers 1¢, 5¢, 10¢ and 25¢

Have the coins in front of you. Hold up a coin for your children and say the name of it, "penny." The children then take the penny and put it in the correct compartment and say its value, "one cent." As they get comfortable with this, you can just tell them the name of the coin and have them find it from the pile and put it into its correct compartment.

Separate the coins by denomination into the different compartments of the money drawer. Show your children a coin and see how many ways they can count to its value. For example, show a quarter and let your children count out 25 pennies, or 5 nickels, or 2 dimes and 1 nickel, or 1 dime and 3 nickels. See if your children can figure out all the ways to combine the coins to make a dollar.

Try a real world test. Next time you go by a vending machine, see if your children can tell you how many of each coin they will need to purchase their favorite snack. If they figure the correct combination, give them the coins to make the purchase.

WHAT IS MONEY AND HOW DID IT EVOLVE?

Silly Store

Playing store is fun and helps children learn the denominations of coins, as well as strengthen their addition skills.

What you will need:

- An empty egg carton for a cash register

- Price tags or stickers

- Several coins in different denominations for each child and coins for the cash register

- Items from around your house that can be "purchased," i.e., toys, canned goods, soap, etc.

Have your children select items from around the house that they would like to "buy" from you, the store clerk. The clerk then determines the purchase price by the age of each child. Preschoolers pay with one coin (a quarter, dime, nickel or penny); elementary school children pay with combinations that increase in difficulty depending on their abilities (for instance, 20¢, 35¢ or 50¢ when young; 87¢, 72¢ or 93¢ as their abilities increase).

What makes the game fun is the personality of the clerk. During each transaction, the clerk (or parent) takes on different personas (such as a bored surfer dude, goofy Valley girl or impatient father of eight).

To make this game more challenging for older children, let your children be the store clerks. Help them determine prices for the sale items and tag them. Next, help them arrange the change in the cash register (egg carton) from left to right in descending order of value. You, as the customer, then choose multiple items to buy from the store, so your children have to total up a sum. You can further test them by paying for your purchases with a bill larger than the value of the item, so your children have to make change.

What makes the game fun
is the personality of the "clerk."

WHAT IS MONEY AND HOW DID IT EVOLVE?

Making Cents

Play makes learning fun! Use this game to help your children understand how many pennies equal each coin denomination.

What you'll need:
- Dice
- 25 pennies
- 10 nickels
- 10 dimes
- 1 quarter

Players take turns rolling the dice. The "bank" pays players a penny for each number rolled. When the player gets 5 pennies or more, he trades them to the "bank" for a nickel, and so on. The first player to get a quarter wins!

YOUR IDEAS AND EXPERIENCES

BANKS AND THE FEDERAL RESERVE

More Than a Candy Store

If your children's only experience with a bank is getting candy at the drive-up window, a trip inside can be a new adventure!

Next time you need to go to the bank, take your children inside with you.

- Take your children to the teller window, ask the teller to show your children a $100 bill.

- Let them watch you fill out a deposit slip or write out a check. Show them where your account number is and explain how the bank uses it.

- Point out the security cameras and explain that they help keep the money safe and that security guards keep the customers safe.

- If you have change, take it in and let the tellers put it through the coin counter so the children can hear it rattle.

- Point out the big vault doors.

- If your bank has safe deposit boxes, show your children where they are and explain that these are where people can keep their very important papers or valuable things.

- Many banks offer special accounts for kids. Talk to a new accounts representative about setting up accounts for your children.

More than a candy store.

BANKS AND THE FEDERAL RESERVE

Adventures of a Bill

How many people will touch or be touched by the dollar bill in your pocket during its lifetime? This activity is not only fun, but also demonstrates to your children how money circulates.

What you will need:

- A dollar bill

- A permanent marker

- A personal computer with an email account

On the bill, using the permanent marker, write "FOLLOW ME. www.wheresgeorge.com."

Go the Web site http://www.wheresgeorge.com and register the bill following the instructions on the site. Be sure to select email notification of when the bill's progress is updated. That way you'll get an email telling you someone else has the bill and has entered information about it.

On your next shopping trip, be sure to take the bill and use it to pay for your purchase, thus putting it into circulation.

When you check your email, you will occasionally get notices telling you that someone has found the bill. You and your children can track how this single bill has traveled in your community and perhaps throughout the world.

THE FUTURE OF MONEY

The ATM Experience

Next time you go to an ATM with your children, let them watch the screen as you punch in your selections. Do not, however, give them your PIN number. Talk to them about the choices as you make them. Be especially sure to point out that you have to choose between the "From Checking" or "From Savings" options and explain that you have to have the money to cover the transaction in whichever account you choose.

This is a good time to explain that you can use any ATM to receive money. If you use one from outside of your bank's system, you will be charged a service charge, which means even more will be taken out of your account than the amount you requested.

Request a printed ATM statement and show it to your children. Have them help enter the withdrawal in your check register and file the receipt when you get home.

THE FUTURE OF MONEY

Become an ATM

Although money in an ATM is readily available, it isn't "free." After this activity, your kids will better understand how an ATM works.

Become an ATM needs a group of at least three to play. They need to be old enough to do basic subtraction and to count money.

You will need:

- A box big enough for a child to sit in
- Scissors – to cut a slot in the box
- Play telephones, walkie talkies or even two juice cans with string to represent a phone
- Play money (borrow from board games)
- Two pads of paper and pencils

Assign the following roles to the participants:

- Customer
- ATM
- Banker

The ATM child gets to sit in the box and will have play money and one of the telephones. The banker will have the other telephone, one pad of paper and a pencil. The customer will also have a pad of paper and pencil.

Start the banker off with a total balance amount for the customer written on his pad of paper. The customer writes how much money he wants on a piece of paper and puts it in the slot of the ATM box. The child in the ATM box will tell the customer "Wait just a minute, please."

He then calls the banker on the phone and says, "(Customer's name) would like to have (money amount on paper). Can he get that much?"

The banker will look at the total amount for that child and subtract out the amount desired. If there is still a remainder, the banker will tell the ATM on the phone, "yes." If there is not a remainder left, the banker will tell the ATM "no." If the ATM gets a "yes" from the banker, he then counts out the amount in play money and gives it to the customer through the slot.

YOUR IDEAS AND EXPERIENCES

YOUR IDEAS AND EXPERIENCES

Money Values

Become a Chief Financial Parent

Money Talks – And You Listened • Money Values

Your Starring Role as a Money Model

Bringing Your Values to Life • Who Needs It? Who Wants It?

Talk is Valuable and a Great Investment

As CFP, your role goes far beyond pure information,

you need patience, flexibility, creativity and humor.

This chapter explains your role as CFP (Chief Financial Parent) and guides you into exploring your own financial history. The more you understand your own money "heritage," the better you're able to be a financial role model for your children. Every day, whether you're aware of it or not, you are teaching your children about money. So you might as well teach them something you believe will be inspirational and motivational.

Here is some of the beneficial information in this chapter:

- **BECOME A CHIEF FINANCIAL PARENT. Whether you are thrifty or a spendthrift, a business owner or an employee, you are, by default, a CFP – Chief Financial Parent.**

- **MONEY TALKS – AND YOU LISTENED. Explore how the stories you heard growing up affect your current attitudes about money.**

- **MONEY VALUES invites you, as a parent, to explore your own values – these are the values about money your children are absorbing.**

- **YOUR STARRING ROLE AS A MONEY MODEL helps you become aware of the unspoken messages you might be delivering.**

- **BRINGING YOUR VALUES TO LIFE shows you how to reflect your true values about money by rewarding your children with things other than money.**

- **WHO NEEDS IT? WHO WANTS IT? prepares you to think about needs versus wants.**

- **TALK IS VALUABLE AND A GREAT INVESTMENT gives you easy tips on discussing money with your children.**

Discover which ancestors have formed your family financial history and how they did it.

Become a Chief Financial Parent

"If you don't talk to your kids about money, who will?"

James Stowers

The moment you became a parent, you also became your children's main resource, guide and teacher of financial education and responsibility. That means, whether you are thrifty or a spendthrift, a business owner or an employee, an artist or an administrator, you are, by default, a CFP – Chief Financial Parent.

"I don't know enough," many parents protest. "I haven't even gotten my own money act together."

In reading this book you've already taken an important step in gaining the information you need to educate your children financially. You're gaining the knowledge you need to help shape your children's financial future. As you read, you'll be surprised at how much of your family's history, as well as your daily monetary dealings, will add to this education. The rest, you and your children can find out together – by enjoying the Ability activities, by asking questions and searching together for the answers and by discussing everyday transactions and financial dealings. Your children can learn from you how to make purchase decisions at the grocery store, how to balance a checkbook, what an IRA (Individual Retirement Account) is and in which mutual funds to invest. **The important thing is that you're willing to learn, listen, discuss and lead by example.**

As the CFP, your role goes far beyond pure information. You need patience, flexibility, creativity and humor. You need to know your child and yourself. Why not share your stories? This will help your children create their own value system and relationship with money.

If you feel your own money management skills need improvement, don't hesitate to tell your children that you're still learning. Coach them that children can learn what not to do, as well as what to do, from their parents.

Money Talks – And You Listened

In your attempt to be a good CFP, it's important to understand your own beliefs about money. This exercise lets you explore how the stories and rules about money you heard growing up affect your current money attitudes. The more you understand the principles you learned growing up, both spoken and implied, the better your chances of communicating them to your children. Jot down the answers to these questions so you can compare and share them later with your spouse, siblings or children.

- What are your family money stories? Include the hardships family members may have endured and their financial successes. Were they business owners or did they work for others?

- What money stories did you hear from or about your grandparents?

- What stories did your parents tell you about the cost of living when they were growing up?

- What advice, warnings or rules did you absorb from listening to family stories about money?

- What money-oriented advice did your parents give you?

- What did your parents' actions show you about money?

- What ancestral money habits did you inherit?

What ancestral money habits did you inherit?

After reading through these questions, you may find you have more to learn about your family's money history. Visit your grandparents, parents, aunts, uncles or siblings and start asking questions. Bring your children along so they can hear and participate in the discussion. Consider video or audio taping your talk so future generations can explore your family's financial tale (often, these discussions will go well beyond financial information and you'll learn a whole lot more about your family history). Discuss what you've learned and write down the stories that made the biggest impressions on you. Is there a theme to these memories? Notice which of these stories have helped you and which have not.

A Grandmother's Inspiration

While walking with my father one day, he pointed out a modest home in our neighborhood and said that when he was younger his mother had offered to buy it for him. When I put this story together with other ones I had heard about my grandmother, I realized that she, a German immigrant, had dealt in real estate at a time when most women did not. She has always inspired me to make the most of my opportunities which have been much more numerous than hers.
Carol, mother of eight

How much ancestral money baggage do you carry?

Money Values

Once you've explored the family history that contributed to your attitudes about money, consider how those attitudes are affecting your children today. Your children are watching you and learning from your example. Are you showing them your true money values? **Money has a distinctive place and purpose in each family.** This is your opportunity to explore and define the role of money in your life.

Money is a multi-dimensional, emotionally charged, limited commodity and a means of exchange. Some believe we exchange money for time. Others think money is one of the means to happiness; if only we had enough of it, life would be perfect. Money can give us a sense of security, but at the same time, the pursuit of money can keep us away from what we value and love most.

You may not be aware of your own money values. Your money values may be hidden within you. Your goal is to realize they exist and understand how they control your actions and decisions.

What do you want from money? Are you chasing the right things? It's important to understand your own money values because these are the money values your children are absorbing every day.

Your Starring Role as a Money Model

Today, whether you tried to or not, you probably taught your children something about money. You taught them by your actions, attitude and responses. As a CFP, you are "on stage" more often than you may think.

That's why it is so important to train yourself to pay attention to your words and actions and consider what they are saying to your kids about money. Ask yourself what your kids are learning about money right this minute. If you're not paying attention, they may be picking up some negative money values.

It's not always easy or fun for you to take the route you'd like your children to follow, but consider how your children might benefit from these positive examples:

- Put aside some money every month in your savings account for a family vacation (or planned "splurge"), rather than pulling out your credit card to charge it. Try to live with as little credit card debt as possible.

- Pay yourself first,® or set aside investment money before paying your monthly bills in order to secure your children's education and your retirement future.

- Show compassion and how money can be used to help others.

- Be thoughtful with your purchases; consider whether or not you are receiving good value for your money.

- Continue to increase your knowledge through study and experience.

Remember, if you have young children, they are watching you for clues as to what money means and how to use it. If you have older children, they may be watching more critically. So when you catch yourself in the act of setting either a good or bad example, don't hesitate to talk to your children about it. You may be surprised at how helpful they can be in suggesting where to cut back in order to save for a family vacation, or what worthy causes deserve your family's support.

Perhaps you want to earn your money through innovative thinking.

Pay Yourself First ® is a registered mark of American Century Services Corporation.

45

Bringing Your Values to Life

"No one knows what the future has in store – each of us must understand our own values, so we can better understand our options for guiding and protecting our family."

James Stowers

I always seem to

have enough.

Another reflection of how you value money may appear when you reward your children for a job well done. For instance, an exceptional report card may be rewarded with cash. However, when money becomes your only reward, consider whether this places too much emphasis on money in your children's eyes. Do your monetary rewards to your children reflect your true values? If not, try rewarding your kids with things other than money. See how your family values can enrich your reward system.

For example:

- If you value friends, give your children extra chances to be with their friends as a reward for a special achievement or outstanding behavior.

- If you want to emphasize the value of family, give your kids extra long-distance minutes for family phone calls. Or reward them with a family outing.

- If you value culture, give your children tickets to a play, musical event or movie they will enjoy.

What are some personal examples of non-monetary rewards your own children may value?

_____

_____

_____

_____

There are endless possibilities beyond money to show your children that you're proud of them. Sometimes, words of praise are all the reward they need. Chances are that the family values you instill when you reward creatively will mean a whole lot more to them than money.

Who Needs It? Who Wants It?

"If you are going to help your kids achieve financial independence, help them understand the need to control their wants. Runaway wants get in the way of financial responsibility."

James Stowers

Most people earn a certain amount of money and, unfortunately, many people have wants and needs that stretch beyond their income. How do you decide what is a need (something you must have to live) and what is a want (something you would like to have)? How do you prioritize these needs and where do your wants come in? How do you guide your children through this process? As a parent, you play a vital role in helping your children understand their options and set their priorities.

MONEY MATTERS

Some families consider money as a tool. They don't worship it, but think it's nice to have. Money is the tool they may use to buy time off or to help organizations they value.

Young children don't always understand where money comes from.

Young children in particular don't always understand money, where it comes from and what it does. Yet all kids have wants and needs that involve money. Retailers are talking to our children every day, trying to persuade them that they need their products and services. **If you, as a parent, don't talk to your children too, you may send them out into the consumer world unprepared.**

Take the opportunities, when your children say, "I want this toy," or "I need this pair of jeans," to discuss the differences between a want and a need. Talk about whether your children feel the jeans are necessary because they have outgrown their clothes (therefore, a "need"), or whether they're desired because the jeans are the cool brand that all the other kids are wearing (obviously, a "want"). If it's determined that your children "want" something, have them help you decide if the resources are available for the purchase. For instance, have they saved up enough of their allowance or are there jobs available that may help them earn the resources needed?

 CFP TIP

ENCOURAGING RESOURCEFULNESS

One way to help create financially aware children is to teach them that wealth is not only tied to money, but also to the resources they develop over time. Such as:

- *Material resources – things they can see or touch, such as clothes, cars and computers.*
- *Non-material resources – things they cannot see or touch, such as knowledge, skills, health and creativity.*

You and your children can create a list of assets you each have – encourage your kids to understand the value of their non-material resources. The goal is a full, rich, contributing life – regardless of how much money they have.

Talk is Valuable and a Great Investment

Many parents agree that talking about money is easier than talking about sex with their kids. It just doesn't occur to parents to talk about money. We are too busy, we don't want to worry our kids, and we really don't know what to say or when to say it. The trick is to make it fun, energizing and interesting to discuss money with your kids. Your conversations can benefit them now and in the future.

The good news is that kids are curious about money. Wouldn't it be a great start to tell them what you're doing with your money?

Here are some general tips for money **TALKS:**

Act casually when talking about money to your kids.

Talk to your kids about money as early as possible. Even letting young children feel or pay for something with a dollar bill will help to give them the idea that those green things in their parent's wallets mean something.

Act casually. Money is just another conversational topic, such as sports, the weekly schedule or what's for dinner.

Leave money in its proper place. Don't let it dominate your value system.

Know your audience. Direct your conversation about money to each child's age and interest. Draw them into a talk about money in a way that is meaningful to them. Use stories from your own life.

Sprinkle questions throughout your conversation and listen carefully to the answers. Everyone loves attention. Your questions and attentive listening give your children a sense of acceptance and deepens your family bond.

MONEY VALUES

Abilities

When I Was Your Age... • Family Tokens

The Family That Works Together... • Stick to Your Needs

What I Really Need • You Mean We Have to Pay?

His Junk is My Treasure • Open Their Eyes • Comparison Shopping

What if...We Had All the Money We Wanted

MONEY VALUES

When I Was Your Age...

One of the best gifts you can give your children is the gift of your experience. Children of all ages love to hear stories about when their grandparents or parents were their age, so why not let them do an interview for a family history.

An interview can be as simple as just talking with Grandma and Grandpa, or as complex as creating a video.

The following are some examples of questions your children could ask:

- What kind of work did your parents do?

- How did you get money?

- Did you get an allowance?

- What did you pay for with your allowance?

- What was the first thing you really wanted to buy? Did you get it? How?

- How much did a candy bar cost when you were my age? How much was a haircut?

- How old were you when you got your first job? What was it?

- How much was your first paycheck?

- Did you save or invest money from your paychecks? How?

- What kind of things did you do on a date and what did it cost?

- How old were you when you bought your first car? How much was a gallon of gas?

- How much did you pay to see a movie?

- How much did your first home cost?

- How much did you pay for your mortgage and utilities?

- What did my Mom/Dad do with their money when they were little?

- Did you make any mistakes in spending when you were younger?

YOUR IDEAS AND EXPERIENCES

_____

_____

_____

_____

_____

"When I was your age..."

BRINGING YOUR VALUES TO LIFE

Family Tokens

Try creating a system that rewards your children for exhibiting good values. The use of "Family Tokens" encourages saving and deferred gratification.

Create a family token (you could use craft sticks, poker chips or bottle caps). When you see your children sharing a toy, helping out without being asked, using kind and helpful words or helping a sibling with homework, give them a token. The children then collect and save the tokens, to be redeemed for a reward.

You can make up a menu of treats to choose from. Rewards can vary depending on the ages and abilities of your children. For example, an eight-year-old's reward choices might include:

- Roller skating with a friend … 10 tokens

- A slumber party with up to 3 friends … 15 tokens

- Rent a new video game … 3 tokens

- Stay up two hours past bedtime … 3 tokens

- Ice cream … 5 tokens

YOUR IDEAS AND EXPERIENCES

BRINGING YOUR VALUES TO LIFE

The Family That Works Together...

Studies have shown that recognition of a job well done is as important, if not more important, than a monetary reward. Don't forget to recognize your family for the times they have teamed up to clean out the attic, spruce up the yard or hold a garage sale.

1. Create a list of the jobs family members do without being paid. Beside each, write the amount you would have to pay someone else to do the work.

2. When your children help with something around the house from the jobs listed above, tell them how much money their work is saving the family.

3. After the family has worked well together on a project, give everyone a pat on the back and congratulate them. Talk about what each person contributed to get the job done. Be sure to stress that the job couldn't have been completed successfully without each person's help.

 CFP TIP

Your family can be rewarded for their hard work without a lot of money by having a picnic, a day at the zoo or a backyard cookout.

YOUR IDEAS AND EXPERIENCES

Stick to Your Needs

It is often hard for young children (adults, too) to separate needs from wants. After trying this activity, you may find that you and your children view needs and wants differently.

You will need:

Stickers of two different colors

Using removable stickers of two different colors, go through one room of your house together and put a sticker on items that are "needs," and the other color sticker on items that are "wants." Talk about the items and decide together why the item is a need or a want.

Give your children some stickers and have them place stickers on the items in their rooms. You can also label the items in your room, and then take turns explaining why you labeled the items in that way.

Example: The items in your children's rooms.

Needs	Wants
Bed	Doll House
Chest of Drawers	Tea Party Set
Clothes Hamper	Action Figures

Make a list of things in a room in your house, and together separate the items into needs vs. wants. Pick several items from each list and discuss what life would be like without that particular item.

For a real challenge, try taking away all the "want" items from your room for a week.

Sample questions:

- Could you replace the item with something else?

- Could you survive without the item?

- Now that you've had the item, would you rather have the money for something else or are you pleased with the value of what you bought?

Note: There is a lot of judgment in these activities. Some may argue that the items listed as wants serve a purpose and are, therefore, needs. Others may consider things on the need list to be a want. Use your values to help you with these judgment decisions and try to remain consistent throughout your house.

NEEDS

WANTS

WHO NEEDS IT? WHO WANTS IT?

What I Really Need

When it comes right down to it, we all have a lot more wants than actual needs. This exercise will help your children prioritize what is really important to them.

Have your children create a bulletin board and divide it into "needs" and "wants." They should then decide their top five needs and wants. Have them go through magazines, advertisements and catalogs to collect pictures of what they want and need. Teens should also find prices. They should review it periodically, and make changes, but never have more than five wants on the board at the same time. This can also be used as a form of financial goal setting.

TALK IS VALUABLE AND A GREAT INVESTMENT

You Mean We Have to Pay?

If you feel as though you are always paying for everything, give yourself a break! This exercise lets your kids do the paying (all you have to supply is the money).

When paying for groceries or gas or other necessities, give your cash to your children and let them pay the cashier. It may give your children more ownership of the items, and it may help them realize that you have to give something in exchange for things. It is also great practice for counting and becoming more familiar with money, especially how much it costs to feed a family.

YOUR IDEAS AND EXPERIENCES

TALK IS VALUABLE AND A GREAT INVESTMENT
His Junk is My Treasure

A fun way to spend a Saturday afternoon is to take the family to a flea market in your area. This is a great way to help your kids appreciate that how we value possessions is very individual. They can also learn to appreciate the idea of recycling.

If your children have a particular desire, check out the cost at full price stores first, then check out the flea market to help them understand that second-hand things can be bargains, as well as treasures.

Go home and see what "junk" your children have accumulated that could be another person's treasures. Have several kids in your neighborhood do the same thing and set up their own flea market.

TALK IS VALUABLE AND A GREAT INVESTMENT
Open Their Eyes

Nothing beats hands-on experience for showing kids the reality of how much money is required to operate a household.

When your children reach high school, let them be your money apprentices for a month. As your apprentices, they will do all of the shopping with you and write out the checks (you will still sign them, of course) for every bill needing to be paid – from mortgage, to car payments to utilities.

By the end of the month, your teens will have a much better idea of where the money goes and that it comes in limited quantities!

TALK IS VALUABLE AND A GREAT INVESTMENT

Comparison Shopping

This lesson will save you time and help your children learn the value of comparison shopping for brand names, price, quantity and size.

What you will need:

- Grocery store advertising supplements from your local newspaper

- Paper

- Pencil

Next time you make up your grocery list, ask your children to use your list to go through the grocery advertising supplements to identify:

1. Which store has the listed items on sale

2. Advertised price differences between items

3. Any coupons for the items on your list

Take your kids to the grocery store with your shopping list and coupons. Let them shop for the items on your grocery list, making sure to choose the correct size, brand and quantity. Show your children where the regular price is listed on the store shelves. As the kids pick up each item that has a coupon, have them note the regular price and the coupon price on a pad of paper.

When you get home tally the differences so all can see what the total savings were for the shopping trip (some grocery stores automatically tell you how much your savings were at the checkout line).

The amount you save can be deposited into their savings accounts or put in a kitty for a special family outing such as miniature golf, a movie or dinner out.

You won't have to do this shopping exercise many times before your kids will pick up on the value of comparison shopping.

The amount you save can be put in a kitty for a special family dinner out.

TALK IS VALUABLE AND A GREAT INVESTMENT

What if...We Had All the Money We Wanted

Often we dream that life would be better if we had more money.

Invite your family to discuss this "what if":

What if we had all the money we wanted?

First ask:

How much do you want?

Notice the amounts. Ask why they chose that amount. Explain why you picked the number you did.

How would your life be better tomorrow if you had that money?

Now get specific:

If you had all the money you wanted, what would you do differently tomorrow?

At school?
At work?
At the grocery store?
With friends?
At home?

Add your own specifics here.

_____

_____

_____

What could be difficult about having the money?

What are some things that can't be bought even if you had all the money you wanted?

How would having the money affect you over the next year? Five years?

 CFP TIP

This is a great dinner table conversation. This is also a conversation you can continue in the car.

YOUR IDEAS AND EXPERIENCES

YOUR IDEAS AND EXPERIENCES

The Allowance Experience

FIRST STEP: Preparing to Give an Allowance

Decide on Your Allowance Philosophy

Noticing Allowance Readiness • Determining How Much and How Often

Setting the Allowance Rules

SECOND STEP: Evaluating Allowances

Being There for Your Children • Raising Allowances

Handling Issues and Solving Problems

Performing an Allowance Review

How do you know when

your child is ready for an allowance?

An allowance is a consistent amount of money that you give your children so they can start learning how to handle financial responsibility. It is an inexpensive way to give your children a lesson in money management. Allowances give children a chance to make decisions regarding saving, budgeting, donations and spending. When they make money decisions of their own, they may encounter many of the same financial problems adults face. **The allowance experience can provide hands-on training for a financially responsible future.** But it can raise many questions for parents establishing an allowance philosophy for the first time.

For instance: When should I start? How much? How often? For what? Can I take it away? What controls do I have over it? These are just a few of the questions that occur with the subject of allowances. This chapter introduces you to giving and evaluating your children's allowances. Here are some of the topics:

Kids who receive an allowance tend to save more money than those who do not.

FIRST STEP:
PREPARING TO GIVE AN ALLOWANCE

- **DECIDE ON YOUR ALLOWANCE PHILOSOPHY.** What philosophy best suits you and your family?

- **NOTICING ALLOWANCE READINESS.** How do you know when your children are ready for an allowance?

- **DETERMINING HOW MUCH AND HOW OFTEN.** Get tips for making the allowance decision.

- **SETTING THE ALLOWANCE RULES.** Before you begin, figure out what you expect the allowance to accomplish.

SECOND STEP:
EVALUATING ALLOWANCES

- **BEING THERE FOR YOUR CHILDREN.** What can go "wrong?"

- **RAISING ALLOWANCES.** What do you do when they want more?

- **HANDLING ISSUES AND SOLVING PROBLEMS.** How can you become comfortable with allowance issues?

- **PERFORMING AN ALLOWANCE REVIEW.** Discover if your children are gaining financial responsibility through their allowance experiences.

First Step: Preparing to Give an Allowance

DECIDE ON YOUR ALLOWANCE PHILOSOPHY

Some parents believe allowances should be given without expectations of chores completed, school grades maintained or good behavior. They maintain that children should strive to meet these expectations as members of their families, regardless of whether or not an allowance is being given. Therefore, allowances are given unconditionally, whether chores are done, grades are good or behavior is up to par. Under this philosophy, the entrepreneurial spirit may still be rewarded if children have a special goal and would like to earn additional money. Let them find some useful work around the house and pay them for its completion.

Other parents believe an allowance should be compensation for work done, so children don't get stuck in an "entitlement" mentality. Under this philosophy, expectations should be clear about what work needs to be completed, the quality level expected and within what timeframe before the allowance will be paid. This experience may mirror job situations in which your children find themselves in later years.

Rather than rely on allowances, some parents develop their own system of providing their children money for their needs and wants. This philosophy may be followed due to budget considerations, to encourage the development of work ethics, or to manage the amount of money children can access.

MONEY MATTERS

Kids have access to money whether they receive an allowance or not. Those who do receive an allowance seem to better understand money because they gain more control over it.

What allowance philosophy best suits you and your family? The following questions will help you decide:

1. Do you want to show your children that they must work to earn money?
2. Do you want to control more of the help you receive around the house?
3. Do you feel family chores should be performed without expectations of money?
4. Are you organized enough to keep careful track of chores performed?
5. Are you comfortable with providing an allowance and expecting nothing in return?
6. Would allowances for your children fit into the family budget?

Can your children be expected to keep their money safe?

If you answered "yes" to questions 3 and 5, you should consider offering an expectation-free allowance. If you answered "yes" to 1, 2 and 4, perhaps your children's allowances should be tied to specific chores. If you answered "yes" to questions 1 and 3, and/or "no" to 6, you may consider not providing allowances.

You may find your particular philosophy lies somewhere among the three options. In this case, consider creating an allowance process that is a combination of each philosophy. For instance, you might have certain chores that are expected of your children, regardless of allowance, but also offer extra chores that might earn your children more money when completed.

Whichever allowance philosophy works for you and your family, communicate your expectations to your children and agree on the rules together. Make the allowance experience an enriching learning tool, not a power struggle.

NOTICING ALLOWANCE READINESS

How do you know when your children are ready for an allowance? Allowances have reportedly been paid starting anywhere from age one to young adulthood. Chances are you'll fall somewhere in between. Parents use many criteria to determine when their children are ready to handle allowances. The following are some factors you can use to determine your children's allowance readiness:

1. Do your children understand the value of coins and paper money, and can they count small sums of money?

2. Can your children be expected to keep money safe (in a piggy bank, purse, wallet or jar)?

3. Have your children been asking for an allowance?

4. Have your children been asking you to buy items you would consider "luxury" purchases (such as CDs, designer jeans and expensive tennis shoes)?

5. Are your children ready to understand and practice the disciplines of saving and budgeting?

Chances are that if you answered "yes" to one or more of these questions, your children are probably ready for an allowance. Many experts believe that by the time a child reaches the age of five or six, they are responsible enough to handle the task. Each family should look at their own situation to determine when the time is right for them.

DETERMINING HOW MUCH AND HOW OFTEN

Deciding on the amount of allowance can be a delicate matter. A recent survey reported that the average weekly allowance of children between the ages of 6 and 8 was $4.80. The average allowance of those between 12 and 17 was $16.60.

> *...some parents give allowance increases based on one dollar for every year the child ages.*

The factors used to determine your children's allowance amounts are often similar to those that help you come to a payment schedule. Allowances are paid in any number of different increments, including bi-weekly, weekly, bi-monthly, monthly and sometimes even annually.

Some of the factors you might want to consider when setting the allowance amount and schedule include:

1. **The age of your children.** Usually, younger children have fewer needs for spending money. As children age, their spending increases, as well as their ability to practice some of the lessons they've learned during the allowance process. Therefore, many parents start small and increase their children's allowances as they grow. In fact, some parents give increases based on one dollar for every year of the child's life.

   An allowance schedule may be based on your child's age, experience and maturity level. Because they have greater experience handling money, older children may be better able to budget their money over longer periods of time (such as monthly or annually). Younger children may function better with allowances distributed bi-weekly or weekly.

2. **The purpose of the allowance.** For those parents who choose to give an allowance as compensation for chores, the allowance might be based on how many chores are completed, how well they are accomplished and how timely. In this case, it is important that criteria for payment be spelled out clearly before the process begins. For instance, if Ben is expected to mow and rake the lawn each week, he should be told that if he fails to rake it, he will not receive the allowance allocated for that task.

Expectations should be made clear what work needs to be completed before the allowance will be paid.

In addition, if your children's allowances are used to compensate for chores accomplished, the allowances should be paid immediately after the work is completed in order to reinforce the pay-for-work concept. In this instance, depending on the timeframe of the chores, a weekly allowance may achieve this goal.

*Are you organized
enough to keep
track of the chores
they perform?*

3. **Your own income.** Obviously, your children's allowance should fit into your own budget. When reviewing your budget, remember that your children's allowances can be used to pay for some of the things you're currently buying (such as movies, snacks and some clothing).

4. **The expenses you want your child to be responsible for.** Some parents base allowances on their children's spending needs. They analyze what they want their children to pay for to determine how much allowance is needed. Some items that parents may include in allowance expenditures include:

- Snacks
- School Lunches
- Movies
- Books
- Computer Games
- Toys
- Gifts
- Savings
- Donations

As your children grow older, the spending list can grow too. It may include taxes, travel, insurance and clothes. Discuss this spending list with your children and together figure out these costs.

Once your children's spending lists are completed, examine them to determine if there are any regular payments that must be made. For instance, school lunches may need to be paid monthly. Paying your children's allowances on a schedule will assure there is always money to cover these expenses.

5. **Your organizational skills.** In a busy household, keeping track of who gets paid how much and when isn't always easy. Consider which payment schedule will best fit your lifestyle, and try to keep it consistent. For example, always pay monthly allowances on the first of the month, or for weekly allowances, always on Sundays after weekend chores are finished.

I.O.U.S: KEEPING ALLOWANCES ORGANIZED

At the beginning of the year, give each of your kids a notebook or calendar containing I.O.U.s, one for each allowance owed (52 I.O.U.s if paid weekly, 12 if paid monthly, etc.). Then pick a day (Friday and Sunday are popular for weekly allowances) to give each child an allowance in exchange for one I.O.U. This way, it will be easier for you (and your kids) to keep track of the money coming in and going out.

When presenting your allowance decision to your children, be prepared for some negotiating. Outline the factors that went into your decision regarding how much and when their allowance is to be paid. In preparation, find out the going allowance rate among your children's friends (your children are likely to bring this up during negotiations). Even if you don't want to match this rate, it's a good opportunity to explain how you came to the amount you chose.

SETTING THE ALLOWANCE RULES

Before you begin the allowance, determine what you expect your children to learn about handling and managing money. Here are some questions to answer before handing out the money:

Saving

- Do you expect a certain amount of allowance to go into savings (for long-term goals, such as college)?

- If so, how much? Many parents set this amount as a percentage of the total allowance.

MONEY MATTERS

One survey shows that kids spend an average of $5 per week on snacks.

- For what do your children want to save? Some parents specify savings for college, gifts or big-purchase items.

- Where should your children put the savings? This can be used as a good opportunity to open savings accounts and to introduce your children to your neighborhood bank.

Giving

- Do you want your children to set aside part of their allowance for donations? Many parents use the allowance experience as a chance to stress the importance of helping others.

- If so, how much? Often a percentage of the allowance is set aside to donate at an agreed upon date.

- Are there any restrictions to whom they can donate?

Completing Chores

- If your children's allowances are tied to chores, which ones need to be completed within what timeframe?

  - Do all chores have to be completed at a certain level of quality before your children receive their allowances?

  - If not, will your children receive their entire allowances, or only a portion for the tasks performed?

Allowing Advances

- What is your policy for giving advances?

- What if your children lose their money or overspend?

What if your child overspends?

Outlining Special Circumstances

- Are there any other reasons for which you would alter the amount or stop giving your children an allowance?

Review your answers to these questions with your children before the allowance process begins. If the ground rules have been made clear and are understood, the allowance experience should be successful for all of you.

 CFP TIP

Getting an allowance is a coming of age moment for your child. Celebrate by creating a container in which to keep the allowance.

Second Step: Evaluating Allowances

In the mythical land of "other people's families," the children always manage their money well, always save and give donations. But in your own family, well, anything can happen. One child may not spend a penny. The other may spend everything the first day, and then try to borrow from their sibling.

This is all a normal part of the allowance learning cycle. Your children are getting to explore their money personalities and you are learning more about how your children look at money.

BEING THERE FOR YOUR CHILDREN

Be supportive as your children learn to manage their money. They may overspend. They may not spend at all. Be there to support and help them develop a way of managing money that is responsible, and that works for them. Remember, allowances are a learning experience.

MONEY MATTERS

One of the easiest errors to make is to respond too quickly to your children's requests.

It's important to allow yourself time to think, and to avoid making the mistake of answering "yes" or "no" to an allowance request or question without first thinking about the consequences of your answer.

Any time money is involved, emotions can crawl in.

RAISING ALLOWANCES

If your children insist they need more allowance, have them keep a daily journal of all their expenditures for one week. Then, go over the diary with them. For each expense, ask the following questions:

- Did you really enjoy what you purchased or did you experience "buyer's remorse"?
- Did you really need it?
- Could you have found it elsewhere for less?
- Did you get your money's worth?
- Discuss your feelings about giving them a raise. Then consider whether more money can be earned elsewhere.

HANDLING ISSUES AND SOLVING PROBLEMS

"Frankie promised to pay me back yesterday, but didn't. Now I don't have enough money for lunch."

"The whole class is going to the movies and out for pizza Friday night. I've got to have more money or I'll be left out."

"Everyone else gets their own clothing allowance!"

Any time money is involved, emotion crawls in. When solving allowance issues, consider using the **LAB** approach:

Listen carefully to the money problems your children describe.

Ask questions. Find out what the real issues are. Find out what they really want or need.

Be consistent. Don't be pressured to make changes that don't feel right to you. If you don't know what to do, try getting feedback from other parents.

 CFP TIP

Do not change your child's allowance or give out unscheduled amounts of money or treats at the time a child is pestering you for them. Acknowledge that your child wants to discuss this issue with you, and suggest a time (it could be as soon as after the groceries are put away, or it may have to wait until after both parents have had time to talk about it). Have your child come up with a good reason to support the need for change.

PERFORMING AN ALLOWANCE REVIEW

Because this is a learning experience, schedule time to sit down with your children to review their allowances. Keep in mind that the ultimate goal of an allowance is to help your children learn to manage their money responsibly. Use this review to celebrate their victories (such as successfully staying within a budget for successive weeks or months, saving for a big ticket item or donating an amount to charity). Also discuss ways to improve upon their financial challenges (for instance, overcoming the temptation to spend too much on clothing or entertainment).

> ### MONEY MATTERS
>
> *The ultimate goal of an allowance is to help your children learn to manage their money responsibly.*

The review should be an informal discussion, held whenever you feel an evaluation is in order. You might have your children keep track of a week's worth of expenditures. Discuss whether or not they felt good value was received for the money spent. Is there anything that might be changed in future spending or saving?

The allowance review provides a good opportunity to assess some of the following issues:

Listen carefully to the money problems your children describe.

- **Allowance Amounts.** Is a raise in order, or will the current amount adequately cover expenses?

- **Savings and Giving Goals.** Should more money be allocated toward the future or for donations?

- **Their Savings' Performance.** Are your children's savings accounts offering competitive interest rates or are there other alternatives?

- **Timing of the Allowance.** Does the current allowance schedule meet your children's spending needs?

- **List of Chores.** If the allowance is paid based on chores completed, is the current list of chores working for both parent and child?

Come to the review prepared. Your enthusiasm and positive reinforcement will be all the reward your children will need to continue on the path to a financially aware future. A successful allowance experience is an important way to help get them there.

YOUR IDEAS AND EXPERIENCES

THE ALLOWANCE EXPERIENCE

Abilities

Allowance Tubs

Choosing Chores

Punch It Out

"Checking" Your Allowance

PREPARING TO GIVE AN ALLOWANCE

Allowance Tubs

Keeping a traditional budget can be a little abstract and overwhelming for kids. The use of allowance tubs is a simple way for children to separate how money is to be used while helping them save toward their financial goals.

You will need:

- 3 jars or margarine tubs (kids like to count money, so make it something easy to open)

- 3 colorful labels that can be attached to the margarine tubs.

- Stickers

Create and decorate the tubs to separate your children's allowance. They may wish to create one for savings, one for spending and one for donations.

Here are some ideas for each tub:

Donations

Find images that represent the causes to which your children would like to donate. Glue them to one of the colorful labels.

Savings

Cut out photos of big items your children are saving to buy.

Spending

Attach pictures of friends, games or CDs to labels.

 CFP TIP

If your children have problems "borrowing" from their savings for impulse purchases, an old-fashioned piggy bank that has to be broken open may be a better option.

DECIDE ON YOUR ALLOWANCE PHILOSOPHY

Choosing Chores

Here's a different twist for those whose children's allowances are dependent on chores. Assign a value to different chores that need to be done, and let your children choose the ones they want to do.

- List your household chores with the value of each chore listed beside it. For very young children, you can draw a simple picture beside the chore so they can identify it.

- Let your children choose the chores they would like to perform for the week.

- Make a chart listing the jobs your children have chosen to do each day, along with their "values."

- When each job is completed, mark it off or cover it with a sticker.

- At the end of the week, tally up the amount for each job completed for each child – that is the amount of their allowance.

YOUR IDEAS AND EXPERIENCES

DETERMINING HOW MUCH AND HOW OFTEN

Punch It Out

Parents frequently run into the "I want/need _____" issue with children. Rather than saying "NO!" all the time, give your children some control over their desires by making a card with an allotment of choices for a certain time period.

You can mark out the choices as your children use them. This is a fun way for kids to exercise control of their own choices, yet still be within parental guidelines.

You will need:

- A blank 3x5 card

- A paper punch or marker

Let your children know how many items and how much you will spend per item during the time period. Put their list on the card. As each item is purchased, punch it out or cross it off the card.

Your children can pay any amount above your maximum from their allowance or from money earned by doing extra chores around the house.

The following is an example of a card for a 17-year-old.

CLOTHING CARD – good through May 31				
Jeans	$40	$40	$40	$40
Shirts	$25	$25	$25	$25
Shoes	$45	$60		
Coat	$75			

DETERMINING HOW MUCH AND HOW OFTEN

"Checking" Your Allowance

Often, the biggest problem parents face with allowances is remembering to give them. This activity will help teach your children to write checks, keep a register and manage money. It will also help you remember to give them their weekly allowance.

You will need:

- Paper
- Ruler
- Pen

First, determine your children's weekly allowance and multiply by 52 (the number of weeks in a year). This amount will be your children's current yearly allowance credit.

Next, with the help of your children, design checks and a check register. Enter the yearly allowance credit (determined above) as the beginning balance. Whenever your children need money, they can write out a "check," enter the amount in their register, and subtract the amount from their balance. You then "cash" the check.

To prevent your children from using all of their allowance at once, you are encouraged to lay some ground rules. For example, they can only withdraw up to three weeks of allowance at one time.

YOUR IDEAS AND EXPERIENCES

YOUR IDEAS AND EXPERIENCES

YOUR IDEAS AND EXPERIENCES

Money Ins and Outs:
Achieving Your Financial Goals

Involving Your Children in the Finances of Everyday Life

Developing Your Children's Budget

Home-Based Work and Earning Opportunities

Working for Others

Checkbooks and Balances

Credit Cards and Beyond

Creating a budget helps you feel more in control of the money flow.

Talking about spending and budgeting gives you a chance to show your children how to express their values in the ways they earn, save and spend money. You can work on:

- **INVOLVING YOUR CHILDREN IN THE FINANCES OF EVERYDAY LIFE.** Talking about everyday costs gives your kids a chance to see how money comes and goes.

- **DEVELOPING YOUR CHILDREN'S BUDGET** helps your children create plans to make it from allowance to allowance.

- **HOME-BASED WORK AND EARNING OPPORTUNITIES.** Earning extra money builds character and a work ethic, as well as income. Here are some ways to encourage your kids and get extra help around the house.

- **WORKING FOR OTHERS.** What are the implications of your children working for others? What will they earn and how will your children benefit?

- **CHECKBOOKS AND BALANCES.** When the money is flowing both ways, it's time for them to have a checkbook. Here are some simple "check" lists.

- **CREDIT CARDS AND BEYOND.** Children are exposed to credit cards at a young age. Here's what you can do to help your children develop good credit card habits.

Help your children develop good credit card habits.

Involving Your Children in the Finances of Everyday Life

"You can always spend what you save, but you can never save what you spend."

James Stowers

Show your kids the cost of living in your household.

The presence of a financial plan can help you feel more in control of your money flow. To create your household and personal plan, record your actual or anticipated expenditures on a weekly, monthly or annual basis. Compare this to your income. This type of plan is also called a budget.

If you share your plan with your children, it allows them to begin to understand how money comes and goes, and what choices you make along the way. When creating a budget, you and your children should consider the following questions:

- What do you need to do with your money?
- What do you want to do with your money?
- How do you plan to earn money?
- How do you stay in control and enjoy the whole process?

Most children (and some adults) don't have a good idea of what it costs to live. **By showing your kids the actual cost of living in your household, you are setting a good example of one way to maintain control and responsibility of your money.** Your good example may also serve to strengthen the family by making everyone an integral part of your financially healthy household.

Before you embark on sharing your budget, find your own comfort level. Some parents feel comfortable telling their children all the details of their earnings and spending. Other parents hold back some of these details.

You might consider increasing your children's involvement in budget preparation as they get older. For example, a preschooler could help plan the spending of the daily snack budget for the family. As they grow to elementary school level, your children may help the family arrange their charitable donations, food or entertainment budget for the week. Middle school children could be included in a monthly discussion of clothing and utility costs (including a discussion on why we turn the lights off when we leave the room or why we don't leave the water running while brushing our teeth). By high school, a young person, in preparation for leaving home, should be able to discuss and plan for big-ticket items such as insurance, car or house payments.

Keep your conversations about money relatively short.

$ CFP TIP

The word "budget" tends to be an abstract word, so you might consider using a different term with younger children. For instance, because a budget is a plan on how we trade money for goods and services, and trading is a concept that may be practiced early in a child's life, the term "Trading Plan" may be substituted. The ability to grasp more abstract thinking normally comes around the age of 11.

PROTECTING OUR PRIVACY

Our children are very talkative, open and outgoing. We give them enough financial information so they can understand what it costs to live, but not so much that our neighbors, our mail carrier or their Sunday school class will know what we make and spend.
Ann, mother of four

Getting over my reluctance to talk about money has helped our family so much. As a family, we are not embarrassed to talk about it. But we tell our children this information is private. Lots of people make more money than we do and lots of people make less. We don't want anyone to use money as criteria for liking us.
John, father of two

The Costs of Living: A TACT Approach

Attitude is important in conversations about money. You don't want your children to feel overwhelmed, worried or guilty about the cost of living. You want them to feel curious and interested. Here are some **TACT** tips for a meaningful conversation about the costs of living:

Timing – Have these conversations when you feel alert, positive and hopeful, not when you are worried about money.

Attention Span – Keep your conversation relatively short, a half hour or less.

Concrete Information –The more information you provide, the more interesting you can be. When you're talking about what things cost, have your bills to be paid available so you can share them with your kids.

- Some parents cash their paychecks and actually let their kids stack money on top of each bill. This plainly shows how the money is traded.

  - Other parents use play money to represent their paycheck and "pretend" to pay their bills that way.

  - Some parents talk about costs while their kids help them write checks and pay the bills.

Talking It Through – Leave time for asking questions. You are taking your kids on an adventure and you want to make sure the experience is understandable and rewarding.

Bill paying became sort of a comedic family routine.

From Chore Time to Good Time

When we got our whole family involved, bill paying went from being a dreaded chore to becoming a sort of a comedic family routine. We developed our own family accounting system. My husband and I reviewed the bills and initialed our approval. Our six-year-old son doled out his "funny money" for the amount. Our middle school daughter wrote the checks. Our son stuffed the envelopes and licked them (which got very interesting, especially when he was eating messy cheese snacks at the same time). I stamped and put the return address on. Paying bills as a family activity helps me pay more attention to our spending and lets the kids be part of our household operations.

Suzetta, mother of two

Family Bonding Through Spending

Another way to involve your children in family budgeting and spending decisions is to include them the next time you decide on a major purchase. After presenting the details of the proposed purchase (cost of the item, as well as the advantages and disadvantages of ownership), let them help you decide if you can afford it. Let them see that all spending has its trade-offs. As a family, answer the question, "What else could we do with this money?"

Making spending decisions together will help strengthen your family. If you are having financial problems, explain that spending has to be cut back. All too often parents try to shield their children from this sort of problem. But children are likely to sense that something is wrong and may see themselves as the cause. Being open, without putting too much of the responsibility on your children, will help raise everyone's cost consciousness and helpfulness.

Parents often try to shield their children from financial problems.

MONEY MATTERS

There are times in most children's lives when they seem to care little about money or are careless with it. For these children, wait until they want extra money for some "must-have" thing then help them create a financial plan for getting their current heart's desire.

Developing Your Children's Budget

In order to make it from allowance to allowance without running out of money, your children need to create a plan. This plan is called a budget. A good budget is simple, flexible and easy to track. You and your children can use the following method for developing a plan together.

Income. What money is coming your children's way? Do your children receive an allowance, earn money from chores or work outside the home? Do they expect gifts of money for birthdays or accomplishments? List only income that's a sure thing.

Owed. What part of your children's income is owed for expenditures or to others? For instance, do they pay for their own school lunches, entertainment, snacks or clothing? Include monthly responsibilities such as donations and savings.

Unusual, Unpaid or Unbilled Expenses. What holiday is coming and whose birthday is next? Make a list of all expenses that don't normally occur every month.

Once everything is listed, simply subtract the amount owed and unusual expenses from income. The difference is money that can be used for savings, investing for long-term goals (like college) or for special purchases. You may even want to do all three. Remember, this same budgeting process can work for you, as well as your children.

 CFP TIP

Writing out a budget lets your kids see money as a limited commodity. It also points out the relationship between income and spending.

Setting Goals

Along with seeing all available options for money, budgeting also helps your children set goals. When budgeting, your children may find opportunities to reach for some of the following goals:

- Saving for something special.

- Regularly saving, investing or donating a certain percentage of their money.

- Earning more money.

- Working just enough to cover expenses, while still enjoying lots of spare time.

Many parents are surprised at how interested their children are in financial goal setting. This doesn't mean you want your kids giving up their childhood and working like Wall Street wizards. But by talking about financial goal setting, you give your children a chance to explore their financial ideas and desires. Some kids will be naturals at setting and meeting such goals. Others will have little inclination to follow through. Encourage your children to pursue goal setting at their own interest level.

When helping your children set their goals, keep in mind that the best financial goals contain the amount of money to be saved, invested or earned; the period of time in which to do it; and the way to reach the goal. Support your children along the way, but allow for the possibility of mistakes and changes. It's all part of the learning process.

Financial goal setting doesn't mean you want your kids to give up their childhood to become Wall Street wizards.

Setting the Goal, Then Letting Go

When our children want something, we have them set a goal. Each month they make a list of everything they want to buy. Thirty days later they can use their allowance to buy something from the wish list. Often, they no longer want the items. Having that month really makes a difference in spending desires.

During the waiting month, they can do research on items they think they really want. When one son wanted roller blades, we comparison-shopped on the Internet. We went to sporting goods stores, knowing we were there just to look and analyze roller blades. This satisfied the urge to be a consumer but without spending.

I do the same thing. If I'm having a real urge to buy books, I'll go to an Internet bookseller and fill the shopping cart. Then I go to the library and request the books.
Jodi, mother of two

 CFP TIP

Setting financial goals can inspire setting life goals. In addition, working through this learning process helps your children gain the confidence needed to successfully function in the financial world. This confidence can help to relieve some of the anxiety children sometimes feel about growing up.

MONEY MATTERS

If you absolutely have to have something you don't need, wait one hour for every $10 of purchase price. You'll be surprised at how often the desire goes away.

Budget Management

With a budget, you are giving your children a chance to manage money or to mismanage money and learn about the complexities of money in everyday life.

Set up a regular review of your children's budget (timed to when they receive their allowance) to evaluate how their money is being managed.

Here's what a budget review can do for your kids:

- Lets them examine their actual spending.
- Shows them areas of spending that need changing or more thought.
- Inspires them to think of ways to increase income or decrease spending.
- Helps them become financially aware and feel more in control of their lives.

But you don't have to be moving faster than a speeding locomotive to get a budget derailed. Any impulsive spending can upset a carefully planned budget.

One method of preventing the budget derailment is teaching your children to prioritize their wants. To decide which of their wants is most important (when there is not enough money to pay for them all) it may be helpful to place a personal value on each want and rank them in order of priority. For instance:

Wants	Value to You
Name Brand Tennis Shoes	Fitting In
CDs	Entertainment
Concert Tickets	Socializing
Jewelry	Impressing Others

Once your children's wants are listed and prioritized, it can become easier for them to make purchase decisions and set financial goals that will work within their own budget.

It can be fun to spend but spending has to be paid for at some stage.

Perhaps your budget has been derailed at some time. Perhaps you've been swept off your feet by a burning desire to buy and to stretch your own delicate budget. By talking to your children about such situations, you can help them understand more about the ups and downs of earning a living and following a plan.

Just like in your own life, budget slip-ups don't have to spell disaster for your children. Encourage them to learn from their mistakes and celebrate their successes.

Home-Based Work and Earning Opportunities

As their number of wants rises above their income levels and over their budgets, your children may develop an interest in earning extra money. Take advantage of these earning opportunities and turn them into learning opportunities. Help your kids become more aware of how they can earn money.

When you give your children a chance to earn beyond their allowance, you give them a chance to:

- Discover their special abilities.

- Think creatively about ways to earn money.

- Recognize the relationship between time and money – how much time it takes to earn a certain amount of money.

- Increase their problem solving abilities by trying new ways to earn money.

- Contribute more to their clothing, tuition and other expenses of their daily lives.

- Increase their independence so they can save for more expensive items and manage larger sums of money.

- Become aware of the importance of education in reaching their life and financial goals.

Go over the chores with your kids, modifying them for age and abilities.

Curbing Impulse Buying

My daughter asked me, "Mom, can I buy this?" "It's your money," I said. She thought it over and ended up not buying it. It's interesting how having our kids earn extra spending money has really minimized their impulse buying. It also cuts down on clutter around our house.
Darlene, mother of three

Cleaning Up at Home

Helping with housework is an earning opportunity that can work for children of just about any age. Even if you expect some housekeeping chores to be performed without pay (making beds, setting the dinner table, etc.), there are usually some "extra" chores you would happily pay to get done (such as cleaning the garage or dusting the blinds). Make a list of these extra chores and go over them with your children. Modify them as necessary for each child's age and ability.

Of course, your children have a marvelous work ethic and always do everything perfectly, efficiently, the first time through. But just in case they are suffering from temporary imperfection, here are a few situations to think about and answer before you get your children to help around the house:

- What if your children promise to do a chore and don't?

- What if your children don't complete the chore to your satisfaction?

- What if your children do the chore later than it needs to be done?

- What if halfway through, your children ask for the money because something "big" just came up?

When you give your children a chance to earn beyond their allowance, you give them a chance to discover their special abilities.

Something else to think about:

• What if your children exceed your expectations and do more than you ask?

When contemplating the answers to these questions, remember the life lesson you'd like this experience to teach your children. What will your children find when they enter the real work force? What flexibility in pay and work expectations will their future bosses provide? It may be difficult to keep these questions in mind when all you want is for your children to be happy, but helping to form good work habits and realistic expectations could add to their future work success.

List extra chores on the refrigerator, with a price per chore.

 CFP TIP

You are hoping to raise children with good work ethics. As you and your children work through this book, your children may also be developing good self-worth feelings. One of the critical things for children to learn is that they have talents and skills that are needed and will be appreciated in the workplace. To know they have something to offer the world develops confidence and takes a lot of the fear out of growing up.

Price Lines for Chores

What you pay for chores will have to do with your economic situation, your money values, the ages of your children and the complexity of the chore.

Here are some ideas from other families on how they assign and price their extra chores:

• List extra chores on the refrigerator with a price per chore.

• Have children sign up for the chores they want to do.

- Ask the children to bid on payment for extra chores.
- Sit together and work out a price for each chore.

Use one or a combination of these ideas to create a system that's easy and clear to all involved.

 CFP TIP

Create a detailed list of expectations for each chore. This might take the form of a chart the child can check off when completed. It is essential when teaching children to do a good job that they know precisely what a "good job" includes.

Chore Chart

When my sons were five and six, I put together two charts with a list of weekly chores. The youngest one could not read so the list included pictures. These charts were laminated so that their names could be switched every week. It also included a space for a check mark by each chore. On Saturday morning, if all chores were checked, then they got $2.00.

Lois, mother of two

CHORE CHART		
Make Bed	Daily	✔
Clean Room	Saturday	✔
Vacuum	Sunday	✔
Feed Cat	Daily	✔
Feed Dog	Daily	✔
Empty Dishwasher	As Needed	✔
Clear Table	Daily	✔
Trash	As Needed	✔
Recycling	Monday	✔
Cut Grass	As Needed	✔
Clean Litter Box	Daily	✔
Scoop Yard	Saturday	✔
Clean Bathroom	Sunday	✔

From lawn care to dog sitting, some kids are naturals at thinking up innovative ways to make money.

Working Around the Neighborhood

Some kids are naturals at thinking of innovative ways to earn money. Help encourage their enterprising thinking by pointing out opportunities. Starting even a modest business can give your kids skills that will help them in school, relationships and other aspects of life.

Enterprising thinking:

- Increases problem-solving skills;
- Encourages risk-taking;
- Allows for making mistakes;
- Lets kids understand the concept of making a profit;
- Shows kids the difference between product and service-oriented businesses;
- Helps kids become aware of their skills and learn new ones.

Here are some ways you can help your children think about their business:

- What do they like to do? What are their special talents or skills?
- In what ways can they help their neighbors?
- Will they do the work alone?
- How will they spread the word about their business?
- Do they need start-up money? If so, where will it come from?
- What if they don't have enough business? What if they have too much?
- How much will they need to charge to make a profit?

- How will they collect and keep track of the money?
- How much time do they want to spend? Will their business fit in with schoolwork and extra-curricular activities?
- What is their back-up plan if things change?
- Does this business sound like fun?
- What could make it even more fun?
- Do they have enough interest to follow through with the project?

One Good Deed Leads to a Business

We have an elderly next-door neighbor. We often baked sweets and the kids took them over to her. Soon, our neighbor was calling and asking the kids to do chores. Another neighbor asked our kids to watch their dog. They watched the dog and took whatever money the neighbor offered. Then a business-oriented friend suggested our kids create a price structure for dog sitting and dog walking. The kids made flyers, and passed them out in the neighborhood. Suddenly, they had a little business.
Darlene, mother of three

Working for Others

If your children are old enough, they may find it easier and more financially rewarding to work for others – like at the neighborhood grocery, hardware store, shopping mall or restaurant. Before they go out into the work world, answer these questions together:

- How much time can they devote to work?
- How will their job affect their schoolwork? Do grades have to be maintained at a certain level to keep the job?

What is their back-up plan if things change?

Make sure your children understand the difference between what they earn per hour and what they actually receive in net pay.

- What kind of job do they want?
- What do they like doing?
- How much do they want to make?
- What will they do with the money?
- How will they get to work?
- What if they don't like the job?
- Will they still have time to help around the house?
- How will their job affect their social life?

If everyone agrees on the answers to these questions, your children can enter the work force knowing they have your support and a positive first work experience is much more likely.

What You Earn and What You Get

Anyone's first paycheck can be quite a shock. Often the expectation is that you will be taking home all the money you've earned. To prepare your children for that first paycheck, discuss the difference between what they earn, and what they will actually receive in net pay. If you want, show your children the difference between your own gross pay and net pay. Talk about how the difference is being used – for federal, state and local income taxes, social security taxes, insurance and benefits (if applicable). By preparing them beforehand, you can help your children adjust their expectations (and budgets) accordingly.

Checkbooks and Balances

When your children show an interest and have enough money coming in and enough expenses flowing out, consider taking them to get their own checking account. If you feel your children have the discipline and can handle the responsibility, checking accounts can also be a great math-learning tool.

Before opening a checking account, go over the following steps with your children. Depending on your bank, a bank employee may be available to discuss the details as well.

- How to shop for a checking account. Consider each bank's age requirements to open a checking account, minimum balances, its locations and account charges.

- How to make deposits – in person, by mail, direct deposit or through an ATM.

- How to write checks.

- How to record checks.

- How to get balance updates and checking account information.

- What happens if not enough money remains in the account?

Finally, one of the most important lessons to learn about a new checking account is **how to keep it balanced**. A simple formula for balancing the account is usually listed on each bank statement.

If the checking account does not balance, double-check the math. Make sure you've recorded your deposits, checks and withdrawals accurately. This includes ATM withdrawals or deposits, service charges, direct withdrawals or deposits. If you can't figure it out, or believe there is an error, a bank representative should be able to help.

If you can't figure out how to balance your account, ask for help.

CFP TIP

When balancing checkbooks, work closely with your child for the first few months, then gradually withdraw the amount of help you give. You may want to "audit" the checkbook every so often. Your audit will help you keep track of how your child is spending money.

Credit Cards and Beyond

Your children may start receiving credit card applications and offers at a surprisingly young age. If your children are earning money and have used and maintained their checkbook responsibly, you may want to consider guiding them through the credit card experience.

Among the good habits to instill throughout this experience:

- Only use the credit card as a convenience or in case of an emergency when cash is not readily at hand.

- Don't use the card as a loan device to buy things you can't afford.

- Before using a credit card, always make sure there is money available to pay for your purchase.

- Pay off the balance on time each month to avoid finance charges and late fees.

- Keep your credit card information private and secure.

Your children's first credit card will require close supervision and guidance on your part. Credit cards tend to be so convenient that their use can quickly get out of hand. Discuss the consequences of making only the minimum payment and how the credit card companies use finance charges. Keep talking and listening to your children and keep a close eye on their credit card statements. Your vigilance can help create good habits that will keep them financially healthy.

What happens if you don't keep enough money in the account?

CFP TIP

As your children begin to make credit card purchases, suggest they keep their credit card receipts, plus cash in the amount of their purchase, in a special place until the credit card bill arrives. With this method, they are assured they can pay the entire bill when it comes. They will also begin to associate a credit card purchase with a deduction in their cash balance.

When your children start earning more money, consider how you are going to help them learn from their earnings. Some parents increase the financial responsibilities of their children, asking them to buy their own clothes, or help pay for their tuition or extra activities. Some parents expect their children to save or invest a certain percentage of their earnings.

Talk about these issues with your children and choose the approach that best reflects your family's money values.

Learning from Earning

For obvious reasons, our daughter didn't mind how much we spent on items she wanted. She would choose the most expensive outfit or the most elaborate games. But when she turned sixteen, she took a summer job and, almost instantly, her attitude changed. When it was her money, she was very careful to check price tags and make choices. It was an eye-opening revelation to see how much our children care about the money they work hard to earn.

Larry and SuEllen, parents of two

MONEY MATTERS

October 16 is National Cut-Up-Your-Credit-Card Day.™ Use this day to focus on how you think about money and the impact your credit card habits have on your long-term financial success.

From Watching Movies to Making Money

I have always loved movies. My parents encouraged me to learn as much about the medium as possible and to do what I loved. So I found a wonderful way of earning extra money – I'm a film critic with my own column. Here's what I have learned from doing this:

I get recognition for writing about films, which is something I love to do and have done for years on-line. I get to reach a wide audience of readers; it's pretty amazing to think that people I've never met may go see a movie on the basis of my recommendation.

From writing this film column, I've learned that my opinion counts. I've learned that I can earn money doing something I love. I've also learned how to handle money.

Here's my advice for kids and teens: Stick with what you're enthusiastic about and keep getting better at it. Even if you're not able to get a high-paying job based on your passion, the real pay-off is in doing something you enjoy and always learning more about it.

Max, student

Learning from experience.

YOUR IDEAS AND EXPERIENCES

Abilities

Pretend You Are the Parent • **Homestyle Cooking** • **Leaving the Nest**
Time Out for Fun • **Goal Setting** • **Dining Diligently** • **Help Wanted**
Marketing 101 • **Budding Entrepreneurs** • **The Family that Earns Together**
Personal Biography • **Banking at Home Sweet Home**
Check Out Checking

INVOLVING YOUR CHILDREN IN THE FINANCES
OF EVERYDAY LIFE

Pretend You Are the Parent

Tell your children that they are the parent and have to use the (play) money to buy what their family needs and wants. Help them by acting out the child's part (for example, pretend you are dying of thirst when they forget to pay the water bill).

With older children, it might be fun and educational to make a list of things they have to pay for before they can buy what the family wants.

Tell your children that they are the parent, help out by acting the child's part.

INVOLVING YOUR CHILDREN IN THE FINANCES
OF EVERYDAY LIFE

Homestyle Cooking

Kids love to eat. When your teens figure out the cost of a home-cooked meal, they will better understand where your money goes. After comparing the price of a home-cooked meal to the price of the same meal in a restaurant, they will see what a bargain they are getting when they eat at home!

- Have your children pick up a take home menu from their favorite local restaurant.

- Next, have them choose a meal.

- Go shopping for the items necessary to prepare the meal at home. Be sure to keep your receipt to make it easier to remember how much each of the items cost.

- Have your kids figure the cost of preparing the meal for the family. Then have them divide the cost by the number of family members to find the cost of a single dinner at home. Remember, if they only used a portion of any of the ingredients purchased to make the dinner, to figure only a portion of the cost.

- Compare the cost of the home-cooked dinner to the same dinner at a restaurant. In most cases, your children will see a significant difference.

INVOLVING YOUR CHILDREN IN THE FINANCES
OF EVERYDAY LIFE

Leaving the Nest

Teens dream of how they will live once they are
"on their own." This exercise will help them discover the
costs associated with the life they would like to live.

Go through the following list with your children
and discuss their dream lifestyle for when they are on
their own. Help them research the costs associated with
living their dreams. It can be interesting to answer these
questions for yourself and then compare them to your
children's lists.

How much will you pay per month for:

Home

- Rent or Mortgage • Natural Gas (heat)
- Electricity • Garbage Pick-up
- Water/Sewage Treatment
- Telephone (include long distance
  and cellular phone service)
- Homeowners or Renters' Insurance
- Food (groceries and restaurants)

Transportation

- Automobile • Auto Insurance • Gasoline
- Parking • Automobile Maintenance

Entertainment

- Movies, Sporting Events, Leisure Activities, etc.
- Cable TV • Internet Service
- Newspapers or Magazines • Gym Fees

Personal

- Clothing • Savings • Investments
- Health Insurance • Donations
- Personal Services (hair cuts or manicures)
- Personal Items (including toothpaste, soap,
  shampoo, hair spray, deodorant and make-up)
- Laundry or Dry Cleaning

Total your answers. How much will it cost to
live for a month? How much will you need to earn?
Do you think you will need to adjust your dreams?

DEVELOPING YOUR CHILDREN'S BUDGET

Time Out for Fun

Occasionally, your children will have the opportunity to spend the day (along with quite a bit of money) at an amusement venue such as a local theme park, a baseball game or the state fair. These are excellent opportunities to teach them about budgeting.

Before the event:

1. Help your children plan this event and set realistic limits on what they will do and how much they will spend.

   • If someone else is driving, will your children help pay for gas or parking?

   • How much is admission?

   • Will they need to buy lunch? How much will it cost?

   • Will they be buying any souvenirs?

   • Are arcade games available? Will they need money to play?

   • Will they need to rent a locker? How much will it cost?

   • What extra refreshments will they want?

After determining in which activities they would like to participate and their costs, calculate the total for the outing.

2. Discuss how much, if any, of the total cost you will pay and how much will be your children's responsibility. If they will be responsible for any of the cost, talk with them about how they plan to pay for it, i.e. from allowance, from savings or from earnings doing extra jobs or chores. Help them make up a timetable for earning or saving the funds needed.

On the day of the event:

1. Remind them of how much money they have and what it is to cover. Be sure to stress that once the money is gone, it is "gone."

2. Be sure your children have pockets with snap tops, or an otherwise safe and secure way to carry their money.

3. If they will be buying souvenirs, remind them to wait until the end of the day to buy. This will give them a chance to think about whether they really want it, to determine if they are getting a good value by allowing time to comparison shop and

will also save them from having to carry the purchases all day long and risk possibly losing them. Remind them that often items sold as souvenirs are available at local department or discount stores for a fraction of the price.

 CFP TIP

If your children run out of money, but still want to buy more, don't give in to their pleas for more money or for you to buy it for them. This will teach them a lesson about budgeting that will last a lifetime!

YOUR IDEAS AND EXPERIENCES

Be sure your children have a safe and secure way to carry their money.

DEVELOPING YOUR CHILDREN'S BUDGET

Goal Setting

Spend time talking about and setting goals with your children. Help them set both long- and short-term goals.

To get you started, here are some questions to ask your children:

- What are your long-term financial goals?

- Do you plan to go to college?

- How are you going to reach your goals?

- Do you currently have a job, and if so, are you satisfied in your position or can you handle more responsibilities?

- How can you get more responsibilities at work and with that, more pay?

Talk about their goals. Are they simple and attainable while still giving them room to grow? Have them write down their goals and put them someplace where they can look at them frequently and change them when necessary.

Long-term example:

Goal: Save to buy a car.

I earn $200 per month.

I spend $100 per month, so I can start saving $100 each month.

If I want to buy a car in the $2,000 range, I will have to save $100 per month for 20 months (1 year and 8 months).

As a parent, you might ask:

- Is 20 months a reasonable time frame to save for a car?

- Are there things you can do to save more?

- Have you considered taxes, car insurance, repairs, replacement of parts, tires, etc.?

Short-term example:

Goal: Save for a new CD.

I receive an allowance of $20 each month.

I spend $15 per month, so I can save $5 per month.

If I want to buy a CD that costs about $15, it will take me 3 months to save enough.

DEVELOPING YOUR CHILDREN'S BUDGET

Dining Diligently

Dining out is not just for grown ups any more! By setting a limit and teaching your children early how to choose wisely from a menu, you will not only be giving them a lesson in budgeting, but may also save yourself the embarrassment of your children ordering lobster when you only have money for chicken!

1. Before entering the restaurant, determine your price limit per person and let the children know how much they can spend.

2. Children's menus are often available for ages 12 and under. If offered, go over the menu selections with your children, and let them choose their dinner. Be sure to point out to them how much their dinners cost, if they include a drink or dessert and if the cost is within your budget.

3. If your children are old enough to order off the adult menu:

Challenge your children to select their meals while staying within the budgeted amount. Show them that not everything they will want is necessarily included in the price of the meal. Do drinks and refills cost extra?

What about a salad? Is one included with the meal, or is it available a la carte? Are lunch portions (or smaller portions) available at a lower price at supper for the asking?

4. See if they can estimate the cost of their meals by rounding each item to the nearest dollar and then adding up the total. Will they be able to stay within their limits?

5. While waiting for your dinners to arrive, make it a game for your children to try to estimate your total bill.

6. When the bill arrives, see if your older children can figure the tip.

HOME-BASED WORK AND EARNING OPPORTUNITIES

Help Wanted

Next time you could use some help for a special project, consider hiring your children. It's a good way for kids to learn new skills, get work experience and earn extra money.

- Create a "Help Wanted" sign for your special job, including what will be required, the time by which it must be completed and the pay.

- Hang your sign on the refrigerator door or other high-traffic area of your home.

- If your children want to "apply," they must ask you for the job.

- Go over the specifics of the job with your children, listing every detail of how you expect the work to be done.

- After the work has been completed, inspect the job. Allow them to improve on any areas you feel aren't "up to par." Remember to keep any criticism constructive. That way they can learn from their mistakes and will be anxious to help the next time you have a special project posted.

- Praise your children's work as you pay them for completing the job.

HOME-BASED WORK AND EARNING OPPORTUNITIES

Marketing 101

When children are eager to work around the house for money, encourage them to make up their own ads to convince you to "buy" their services. Ask them to tell you exactly what they will do and how much they expect to be paid.

YOUR IDEAS AND EXPERIENCES

_____

_____

_____

_____

_____

_____

HOME-BASED WORK AND EARNING OPPORTUNITIES

Budding Entrepreneurs

Kids love to make or grow things themselves. And, it really gives them a sense of pride when someone is willing to pay for their efforts.

Next time a garage sale takes place in your neighborhood, let your kids set up a concession stand on your driveway. Some ideas for sales items include:

- Lemonade
- Cookies
- Home-Grown Vegetables or Fruits
- Soft Drinks or Bottled Water on Ice
- Craft Items

Be sure they take into account all costs involved, (such as lemonade, cups, sugar and ice) and help them come up with a sale price which will cover costs and make a profit.

HOME-BASED WORK AND EARNING OPPORTUNITIES

The Family that Earns Together

If your family shares a common goal such as a vacation or adding a backyard pool, why not raise money as a team?

1. Determine your family's goal. Discuss it as a group, and build excitement by letting family members get brochures, cut out ads, and do research on the Internet. Then state your goal in writing, describing it and including how much it will cost. Post your goal on the refrigerator.

2. As a family, decide how you will raise the money necessary to reach your goal. Some ideas are: have a family garage sale or collect aluminum cans to take to the recycling center.

3. Assign one family member the task of depositing the money in a savings account and keeping the family informed of the balance and how much more is needed to reach your goal.

Additional ways to add to the fund:

1. Let family members contribute extra change, found money (such as money from the washing machine) to a coin jar.

2. See how much lost money you can find. Watch for coins on the street, under the bed, in the couch or left in vending machines.

3. Take your own snacks when you go places. Put the money you save in the account for your special project.

4. Become avid coupon clippers. Designate half the money you get back on coupons as money for your special project.

5. Dine on home-cooked meals instead of those from restaurants (try making your own pizza instead of delivery). Add the money you saved to your special fund.

WORKING FOR OTHERS

Personal Biography

Filling out an employment application or writing a resumé can be a daunting task. Start when your children are small to help them identify their strengths and skills.

When children are as young as three years old they have already accomplished a great deal and they love to talk about it. You can use a small poster board and markers to list their accomplishments such as going potty, doing a somersault or running fast. You can even add some things they are trying to do and make space to check it off when they do it.

Older children can keep track of their accomplishments in a journal. This activity gets them to keep track of what they have done. If they continue to work on their journal, they will have lots of information they can use when they need to impress a future employer.

To prepare teens for adult life, their personal biography can take the form of a resumé. Spend some time helping them put together their resumés, remembering to emphasize the talents they can offer a prospective employer. It should sum up all of their work, including their volunteer, educational and community experience.

This information can be useful for your teen to review when preparing for an interview, as well as for potential employers, college admissions and scholarship applications.

When applying for a job, it is beneficial to research the companies to which they are applying. They can then modify their resumé to demonstrate how their experiences fit the employers' needs.

CHECKBOOKS AND BALANCES

Banking at Home Sweet Home

By creating your own bank at home, your children will learn in a caring atmosphere the art of controlling their spending and managing a checking account. That way when they are old enough, they will know how to handle a real checking account.

Here's how it works:

You are the banker.

- As banker, you will keep your children's cash, make a record of their transactions, cash their checks and give them receipts for their transactions.

- If they have insufficient funds, you can return (or bounce) their checks.

- If you feel they are spending too freely, adopt a policy of requiring two days' notice before making a withdrawal.

- If you desire, you can encourage saving by offering to pay interest.

Here's how to get started:

- Create a bank in which your kids can deposit their allowance, complete with receipt books, checkbooks and deposit slips. You can use old checks and check registers, or have fun helping your kids create their own.

- When the kids want to spend money, let them write a check to you. Make sure they enter the amount of their check in their check register.

- Show your kids how to keep a running balance of their accounts.

If they have insufficient funds,

you can return their checks.

CHECKBOOKS AND BALANCES

Check Out Checking

Your children are ready for checking accounts when they start earning a paycheck and certainly need one when they are ready to go to college.

Some banks offer checking accounts only after the customer is old enough to have a driver's license; others will open a checking account for a child as young as 13, as long as a parent is on the account with them. Call several competing banks in your area to get information about opening a checking account. You will find that each offers its own variation on the traditional checking account with its own minimum balance requirements, service fees and other stipulations.

To compare, ask the following of your banker:

- What is the minimum age to open a checking account?
- What kind of age documentation do you require?
- Do your checking accounts earn interest? At what rate?
- Do you have a minimum required balance? What is the fee if the account dips below the minimum?
- What is your lowest service charge?
- Do you charge extra for checks?
- Do you return checks with the statement?
- What are your charges to stop payment on a check?
- What do you charge for returned checks?
- Where are your branches located? Can I conduct transactions at any of them?
- Are debit cards available? What charges are associated with them?
- Where are your ATMs located?
- Can I access my account on-line?

After your children choose a bank and open their accounts, be sure they enter all of their checks in their check registers as they write them. Help them balance their accounts promptly after their statements arrive the first few months or until they get the hang of it.

YOUR IDEAS AND EXPERIENCES

YOUR IDEAS AND EXPERIENCES

Putting Your Money to Work

Earn money while you sleep.

Y ou and your children may dream of earning money while you sleep. However, before this can happen, you need to set aside some money to invest. The first step in the investment process is saving. This chapter will show you how to help your children create a nest egg for investment. You'll also see how time and money work together.

- **WHY SAVE MONEY? explains the benefits of getting your children involved in saving money.**

- **THE SHRINKING DOLLAR shows how money, left alone, could eventually lose value over time.**

- **HOW TIME AND MONEY WORK TOGETHER. Your children have time on their side as they begin to understand the magic of compounding.**

- **BANKING ON SAVINGS gives your kids some things to consider before putting their money in a bank.**

- **MONEY MARKETS, CDs AND OTHER SAVINGS INSTRUMENTS. Once your children are in the habit of saving, show them other alternatives.**

Savings account to the rescue.

Why Save Money?

To help you understand what motivates kids to save money, we asked some children to share their reasons for savings. Here's what they told us:

To Buy Stuff. The bike of their dreams costs more than $200, but they only get $10 a month in allowance. Without saving, those kids will be walking everywhere. By saving, larger purchases become affordable.

To Do Things, NOW! "Everyone" just decided to go to the amusement park. Unfortunately, this week's allowance was spent a long time ago. Savings account to the rescue! By having some money set aside, children can satisfy some of their immediate gratification needs.

*The
Shrinking
Dollar.*

To Do Things Later. Believe it or not, children also set long-term financial goals. Teenagers will often start saving for a car years before they can drive. Imagine the pride (yours and theirs) in knowing they have the discipline and self-control to keep money in the bank.

In the not too distant future, your children will be on their own. Because saving money requires discipline and hard work, your children may, at first, resist the idea. That's why now is the time to start them in the habit of saving more than they spend.

The Shrinking Dollar

Beyond having money to spend, there's another reason to aggressively save and invest money. Money, left in a piggy bank, may eventually lose value over time.

We've all heard stories of how in the 1900s, you could have eaten dinner for four in a fancy restaurant, left a generous tip, and received change – all from a single dollar bill. In the mid '70s, you may remember going to your local fast food hamburger franchise and buying a burger, fries and drink for less than a dollar. Today, for the same dollar you can only buy the hamburger (provided you have some extra change for tax). Your children may be able to relate to gumball machines, which used to give you candy for one penny. Now, they take nothing less than a quarter.

On the average, the dollar has continuously lost value since 1900. In fact, if you had a dollar in 1900 and held on to it until today, its buying power would be worth less than five cents.

The only way to be certain your money will be worth tomorrow what it is today is for it to be in a savings or investment vehicle that is earning an annual rate of return greater than the rate of the shrinking dollar. If your children's $10 allowance is left in a piggy bank, wallet, or under a mattress, then a year from now that $10 may only buy $9 worth of snacks, clothing or movie tickets.

How Time and Money Work Together

"It is essential to start saving and investing regularly and early in life."

James Stowers

As the CFP, you are in a great position to get your children interested in making money on their money. This is known as **compounding**. Because they are young, time is on your children's side, and the sooner they get started with their savings plan, the sooner their money will start working for them.

To help your children understand the concept of compounding, let's turn to Mother Nature for a quick lesson. A farmer can plant a **single seed** of wheat, care for it and from it create more than **100 seeds**. If these 100 seeds were planted and properly cared for again, they would produce at least **10,000 more seeds of wheat**. This is the same concept of compounding – money, properly cared for over time, will grow and multiply. Isn't nature a wonderful teacher? As you share this story with your kids, look in your own garden for examples of "natural compounding."

How much money your children can accumulate through compounding depends on two critical factors: time and the annual rate of return. Time is the most fundamental – the longer your children let their money work, the greater their chances are for long-term financial success. By putting their money in investments (more on this later) that can achieve a higher rate of return, the less money they must set aside.

What should you focus on for now? If your children are young, simply getting them in the savings habit is a great start. For teens, discuss and stress the importance of looking for opportunities with higher returns.

Start investing as early as possible.

MONEY MATTERS

The Rule of 72:
To find out when your
investment will double in
value, simply divide the
number 72 by the rate of
return your investment
receives. For example, if an
investment is receiving an 8%
return, it will double in value
in 9 years (72 ÷ 8 = 9).
The higher the rate of return,
the quicker the investment
will double.

To illustrate the magic of compounding, take a look at the following chart:

Compound Results of a One-Time Investment of $100
Compounded Monthly

	10 Years	20 Years	30 Years	40 Years
At 6% interest	$182	$ 331	$ 602	$ 1,096
At 8% interest	$222	$ 493	$1,094	$ 2,427
At 10% interest	$271	$ 733	$1,984	$ 5,370
At 12% interest	$330	$1,089	$3,595	$11,865

This chart shows you how a one-time investment of $100 would grow over time at various interest rates. As you can see, at an average annual interest rate of 12%, $100 would grow to $11,865 in 40 years. If you think this chart will help your children become interested in compounding, wait until you see the next one.

The following chart shows what happens when your children make a one-time investment of $100 and then make a commitment to add $10 each month.

Compound Results of a One-Time Investment of $100 + $10 Monthly
Compounded Monthly

	10 Years	20 Years	30 Years	40 Years
At 6% interest	$1,821	$ 4,951	$10,647	$ 21,011
At 8% interest	$2,051	$ 6,383	$15,997	$ 37,337
At 10% interest	$2,319	$ 8,327	$24,589	$ 68,611
At 12% interest	$2,630	$10,982	$38,545	$129,513

Earning 12% interest, at the end of 40 years, your children would have $129,513. Their total investment would be only $4,900 ($100 initial investment + $4,800 ($10/month for 480 months).

THE FOUR KEYS TO ACCUMULATING WEALTH

1. Start investing as early as possible. It takes significantly less money to accomplish what you want and you have more time working for you.

2. Save on a regular basis. It is an easy way to accumulate wealth.

3. Begin investing with the largest possible sum. You will have more money working for you over a longer period of time.

4. Reach for the highest rate of return that's safe for you. Each additional percent is important. The higher the rate, the less money it takes to accomplish what you want.

James Stowers, from *Yes, You Can...Achieve Financial Independence*

A savings account makes your children more thoughtful and less impulsive about their spending.

Banking on Savings

A savings account can make your children more thoughtful and less impulsive about their spending. If they want their money, it requires a trip to the bank. They can't just open up their piggy bank, grab their savings and dash out to the store.

A savings account at a bank also has these advantages:

• Your children become familiar with the bank and how to use it.

• Their money earns a modest interest. They can see for themselves how compounding helps their money grow.

• Someone other than you has the responsibility for keeping your children's money safe. Plus, it's kept out of the reach of siblings.

• Your kids learn how to interact with tellers and bank personnel.

PROTECTING YOUR SAVINGS

My grandmother ran a tight ship. During the Depression, all of her children pitched in with money they earned to help the family make ends meet. One of my uncles, however, had managed to set aside some money and had hidden it in the heating vent of his bedroom. Unfortunately, he talked in his sleep. When his mother heard him, his secret was out. His hard-earned savings went quickly into the family pot. Remember to keep your savings in a safe place.

Carol, mother of eight

WHERE DOES THE MONEY GO?

When your children make a deposit at a bank, one of the questions you may be asked is, "Where does my money go?" The simple answer for very young kids is, "The bank is going to use it for a while, but they'll give it back when you want to take it out." As your kids get older, you may want to explain to them how they are actually lending money to the bank.

Savings accounts, Certificates of Deposit (CDs) and bonds are actually loans given by you to a bank or institution. In return, you are paid a fixed sum of money (interest). At the end of the loan period, the full amount you lent is returned to you.

Choose a bank that will nurture your children's savings.

YOUR CHILDREN'S FIRST BANK EXPERIENCE

Provide your own story of each child's first experience in a bank, or with their bank account. How did they feel about the experience – the process, the place, the people they met? How did they feel having their own account?

You want your children's first experience with banks to be positive.

TRUE TO FORM SAVINGS

As far as keeping track of money and saving money, our plan for each of our boys is on a form that I made up on my computer. We have them set aside a small percentage for donations, 20 percent then goes toward long-term savings that they cannot touch, and the next 20 percent goes toward short-term savings (camps, retreats, trips, etc.) The balance is theirs to spend as they please. They fought this system a little at first, but I showed them how it's still their money and by saving now, it will be easier for them to do what they want to do in the future. Now, they're comfortable with the savings plan and pay more attention to the way they spend their money.
Bonnie, mother of two

THE BANK CHOICE

You want your children's first experience with banks to be positive. Here are some things for you and your children to consider before selecting a bank. Ask them:

You are trying to show your children that saving money can be fun and fulfilling.

1. Is there a minimum amount required to open a savings account? Some banks have a $200 minimum. Others accept $10. Choose a bank your children can afford.

2. Is there a monthly fee if you don't maintain a certain balance?

3. Can your child's name be first on the account? (As guardian, your name will probably also need to be on the account, but it's more exciting for your children if their name is first).

4. Is the account federally insured? (The FDIC – Federal Deposit Insurance Corporation insures a person's total deposits up to $100,000).

5. Is there a special teller or accounts representative who helps children?

6. What are the best interest rates? Are the rates compounded, meaning, is interest paid both on the principal and accumulated interest?

Once your questions are answered, let your children help you decide which savings institution to use. If your children participate in the selection process, and are happy with their choice, they will be much more likely to save on a regular basis.

 CFP TIP

If you have a savings account, talk to your children about how you use it. If you are saving every month, let your kids know.

Money Markets, CDs and Other Savings Instruments

Although a savings account is an easy, safe place for children to keep their money, an account's interest rate may not be equal to or exceed the rate a dollar is losing value. So, as your children's savings accounts grow, you can introduce them to other options that may offer higher interest rates. These include:

- Certificates of Deposit (CDs),
- Money Market accounts, and,
- Bonds.

TAKING NOTE OF CDs

As we mentioned before, when you "buy" a CD you're not really buying anything, but **loaning money** to the bank for a set period of time. In return, the bank will pay you a set interest amount and then return your entire loan at the end of the period. With your help, your children can easily work with their banker to transfer money to a CD from their existing account. Like the savings account, your name will probably need to be on the CD, too. Keep in mind, most CDs require a minimum deposit.

Many banks will reward your children with a higher interest rate if they agree to loan their money for a longer period of time. Because interest rates vary, you should shop around to find the best deal. Also, make sure your children understand there is a financial penalty (or fine) if they ask the bank for their money back before the end of the time period.

CDs require a commitment.

CDs PLAY WELL

As the children's savings accounts have grown, they have learned more about interest. They have also chosen to use their money to open their own Certificates of Deposit. Our youngest is ten. With my help, he opened his own CD when he was eight. We showed our kids the board at the bank that lists the different interest rates. They were attracted by the higher interest rate. We explained that with a CD they couldn't use that money while the bank was using it. The bank would keep it for the term of the agreement.

Darlene, mother of three

SHOPPING FOR MONEY MARKETS

If your children want to look for a higher interest rate than a savings account, but don't want the time commitment of a CD, a money market account could be a next step for them. Money market accounts are like savings accounts however, they:

- May pay a slightly higher interest rate (the amount will vary depending on the market).

- May limit the number of withdrawals you can make during a month.

- May offer limited check-writing abilities (although your children may not be able to take advantage of this option).

- May require a minimum investment in the account, with the possibility of service fees if funds dip below that amount.

BONDS

With a bond, you are "loaning" your money to a company or entity with the promise of getting it back, with interest, after a set period of time. Your children may already receive United States Government Savings Bonds as gifts. This is really a loan to the government.

Bonds are issued when the government or a corporation wants to raise money to do things. For example, the government might issue bonds to help refinance existing debts, build schools, redo highways or to pursue special projects. A corporation might issue bonds to help raise money to buy another company, to expand their current operation or to get money to buy equipment.

While your children are under the age of 18, they probably won't be able to buy bonds on their own. However, you should be aware of how bonds work. They vary according to:

- **Safety** – Bonds rated AAA (as rated by the Standard & Poor's rating system) are at the high end of the rating scale. The rating measures the bond seller's ability to repay the loan. Keep in mind, if the seller has financial problems, it may not be able to pay interest or return your original investment.

- **Type of institution issuing the bond** – Ranging from private companies to government entities.

- **Length of time you are willing to loan the money** – Short-term bonds mature within five years, while long-term bonds mature in more than ten.

When discussing this savings instrument with your children, it's helpful to note that bonds have not historically protected against the dollar's declining value over time to the extent that stock-based investments (such as mutual funds) have. We'll talk about these types of investments in chapter 6.

Bonds are issued to help the government raise money.

YOUR IDEAS AND EXPERIENCES

YOUR IDEAS AND EXPERIENCES

PUTTING YOUR MONEY TO WORK

Abilities

Saving for Something Special

The Magic of Compounding

Bean Counting

Watch It Grow

Match It/Graph It – 401K for Kids

Getting More for Your Money…Very Interesting

WHY SAVE MONEY?

Saving for Something Special

Saving money is easier and more fun when your children are saving for something special.

To make saving fun, have your younger children start off saving for something relatively inexpensive, so they can reach their goal within a few weeks. Since kids are very visual, try attaching a picture of the coveted item to an envelope and put it in a place that is easy for them

to see every day. Each week, have them put a portion of their allowance into the envelope. When enough money has accumulated in the envelope, take your children to the store and help them make their purchase.

Older children often enjoy making a wish list, which may contain multiple things they are hoping to buy. Help your children create a list of the things they are saving for and the cost of each item. Have them post it in a place that is easily visible every day such as the refrigerator door, the bathroom mirror or their bulletin board. As they save enough to make a purchase, they can cross the item off their list.

 CFP TIP

Occasionally, parents might offer their children an incentive to save. One idea is to offer to help pick up a portion of the purchase price of something on their list if they save a portion. Another idea is to contribute something that compliments their goal, i.e., if they save enough to buy the new bicycle, the parent will buy the helmet.

HOW TIME AND MONEY WORK TOGETHER

The Magic of Compounding

Have you ever seen a magician put one rabbit into his hat, but then pull out two? Something similar happens when you keep your money in a savings account for a period of time. The bank pays you interest and the longer you keep it in, the more your money grows! Try the exercise below to teach your children about how compound interest works.

You will need:

- A monthly calendar
- A pen
- A jar of pennies

Explain to your children that you will show them how a penny, at 100% interest, compounded daily, can grow.

1. Your children will be the depositors. You will be the banker. Start on the 1st of the month. Have them put one penny on the table. Explain that at 100% interest compounded daily, the bank will match the amount of pennies they have saved each day. Then add a penny to theirs. Put a check mark on the 1st on the calendar.

2. Now tell your children that it is the next day, or the 2nd. Ask them to count their pennies (they will have two). Tell them you will compound at 100% interest again and add two more pennies. Put a check mark on the 2nd day.

Repeat step two for each day of the month until you run out of pennies. (You will most likely run out of pennies before the end of the second week.) To fill an entire 30-day month you would need 1,073,741,824 pennies…or over 10 million dollars!

HOW TIME AND MONEY WORK TOGETHER

Bean Counting

Help your children understand how money grows in an interest bearing account, by letting them become bean counters. The hardest part is to resist the temptation of eating away at their savings.

You will need:

- 2 lbs. dry beans or jelly beans
- 1 jar for each type or color of bean

Separate the beans by color or type. Give your children all beans of one type or color to represent their money. Place all other beans into jars, separated by color. Choose one jar to represent the bank's money, or interest. You should have one empty jar.

Place all of the jars together on a table and tell your children that these represent all of the money in the bank. Explain that the different jars represent money that belongs to different people and point out the color that is money that belongs to the bank.

When your children want to put money in the bank, they will be given their own savings account, represented by the empty jar. Have your children add five beans to their account. Go on to explain that after some time, the bank will pay interest on the money in each account. This means that the bank will take some of its own money and put it in their account. At this point, add one bean from the color representing interest to each child's jar.

Of course, your children will add more money to their account jar from time to time. Every time this happens, add another bean from the interest jar to their "account" jar.

At this point, depending on your children's ability to understand, you can explain that as the money grows in the account, the bank will give more money each time because of the way interest works, e.g., if they put 10 beans into their account, then the bank will add two beans from the interest jar.

HOW TIME AND MONEY WORK TOGETHER

Watch It Grow

Young children like to plant seeds and watch them grow. Use this activity to help them understand that one seed, if planted and cared for over time, can turn into many more seeds, just as one dollar, if saved and earning interest, can turn into many dollars over time.

You will need:

- Pumpkin seeds
- A small gardening trowel
- A sunny spot in your yard with plenty of space for a viney plant

Here's what to do:

- Prepare the earth for planting, let your children help dig and loosen the soil.
- Show your child a seed and explain that if left to grow, it will produce many more seeds.
- Let your children tend the plant, making sure it is watered and weeded.
- Watch as the plant grows, remind your children that the plant came from just one seed.

- At harvest time, pick your pumpkins. How many pumpkins did just one seed produce?
- Carve your pumpkins and let your children remove the seeds. Can they count the number of seeds?
- Talk about how many more pumpkins they'd have if they planted all of the seeds.

Be sure to remind your children that just one seed was able to produce so many new seeds because they took care of it and gave it time to grow.

RECIPE: Baked Pumpkin Seeds

Rinse seeds and set on a paper towel for a couple of hours, until dry. Heat oven to 350° F. Sprinkle cookie sheet with melted butter. Spread pumpkin seeds in a single layer on sheet. Bake for approximately 25-30 minutes. Place baked seeds in a bowl, sprinkle with salt, and enjoy eating.

BANKING ON SAVINGS

Match It/Graph It – 401K for Kids

Adults are more inclined to contribute to their retirement accounts when their employer gives them the incentive of matching a portion of their contributions. A reward system in which you match all, or at least a portion, of your children's savings works well with kids of all ages, but especially if they have a big-ticket item for which they are saving.

Why not consider matching a portion of your children's deposits into their savings account? This can be done either for savings in general or for savings toward a specific goal. Determine the percentage you will offer and tell your children that you will match every deposit they make by the determined percentage. It will encourage them to make deposits and you can feel good about helping their savings grow.

You may also find it helpful to create a graph similar to the one on this page. Using colored markers, show your children's deposits, your matching deposits and interest paid by the bank so your children can see their progress and keep a record of their savings.

Molly's Class Trip - $175

MONEY MARKETS, CDS AND OTHER
SAVINGS INSTRUMENTS

Getting More for Your Money... Very Interesting

After your children have accumulated a substantial amount in their traditional savings account, you may want to explain to them that by moving their savings to an account earning greater interest, their savings will grow even faster. To help illustrate this, show them how long it will take their money to double in its current account by using the rule of 72: divide 72 by the interest rate they are currently making. For example, if they are currently making 2% interest, their money will double in 36 years.

Show your children how to check out the financial pages of your local paper to find CD (Certificate of Deposit) and Money Market interest rates from several competing banks in your area. (Children who have accumulated significant savings may want to look into other financial instruments that may produce even higher interest returns). To help them compare and choose the bank that best suits their needs, create a chart similar to the one below listing institutions, types of accounts offered and their requirements. They can then use the rule of 72 for each institution on their chart to easily see in which account their money would double the fastest.

 CFP TIP

When your children have accumulated enough in savings to open a CD or Money Market account, be sure to congratulate them, after all, they have reached a savings milestone. To celebrate this great accomplishment, consider treating your children to a special outing on the way home from the bank.

Name of Bank	Minimum Balance	Time Constraints	Fund Availability	Fees	Interest Earned	Years to Double

YOUR IDEAS AND EXPERIENCES

YOUR IDEAS AND EXPERIENCES

Growing Money Right: Investing

When your children have accumulated a little money,
you can introduce them to the world of investing.

Savings accounts, CDs and money market accounts are relatively "safe" places to keep money...for **short periods of time**. However, because they are tied to a dollar they may not appreciate in value faster than the decline in the value of a dollar. That means, after 10 years or so, you may actually be losing money rather than making money.

Another option to consider is trading your money for something that can grow in value over time and/or will generate income. This is **investing**. This chapter explores some of your children's investment options. As before, because they are under 18 years old, you may have to actually hold the account in your name and do the investing on their behalf. Here's what this chapter includes:

Your kids may have a natural gift for understanding the market.

- **THE INVESTING DECISION gives you tips for helping your kids find investments that are right for them.**

- **OWNING PROPERTY BY COLLECTING gives tips on an investment vehicle that kids may find fun.**

- **YOUR CHILDREN AND THE STOCK MARKET provides the essential facts for talking about and understanding common stocks.**

- **MUTUAL FUNDS OFFER A DIVERSE INVESTMENT discusses mutual fund investing.**

- **BUYING AND SELLING suggests questions to ask before buying or selling investments.**

- **INVESTMENT ATTRIBUTES CHART compares the attributes of various savings and investment options.**

The Investing Decision

"There is no such thing as a perfectly safe investment, free from all risk."

James Stowers

In chapter 5, we talked about **"lender"** investments – savings accounts, CDs, money market accounts and bonds. Now it's time to up the ante and talk about **"owner"** investments. Through owner investments, your children (with your help) have the opportunity to become an owner of property, common stocks and mutual funds.

There are two big differences between lender and owner investments. The first is **risk.** As an owner, you willingly assume a greater degree of risk than when you are a lender. The second is **rate of return**. Because you are willing to take a greater risk, you also have the opportunity to realize a greater rate of return.

It's important to take a minute now to understand the word *risk*. Whether you are a lender or an owner, you assume some risk. Smart people do not seek to avoid risks, but simply try to hold them within reasonable limits. What's reasonable for you and your children may be different than what's reasonable for another family. We all have different levels of risk we're willing to accept.

If you keep your money in lender investments, you risk it losing value over time. There are advantages to being an owner. An owner receives **all** the profits. There is no ceiling on the financial gains you may enjoy (compared with the fixed interest offered by savings accounts, CDs, money market accounts and bonds). But the biggest advantage is that owner investments are free from the shrinking value of a dollar.

Along with the advantages of ownership comes risk. The risks of owner investments include:

- Owners absorb any losses incurred by the investment.
- There are no guarantees of a return on your investment.

- Profits are generally unpredictable.
- There is no guarantee of the value you will receive for the property if you choose to sell.

Patience is key when investing. Time can be your children's best friend. If they get off to an early start, it generally takes less money to reach their financial goals (whether it be a college education, early retirement or financial independence) because their money will be at work for a longer period of time. Time also allows them to overcome errors in judgment along the way.

Investments can earn money the following ways:

- **Appreciation** – They increase in value over time such as baseball cards, stocks or real estate.
- **Dividends** – Income received as an owner of a business.
- **Capital Gains** – Profits received from the sale of assets.

You want an investment that your children can easily purchase in small increments.

At the end of this chapter (page 170) is a chart that compares the attributes of the different ways your children can save and invest. To help you better understand these concepts, take a couple of minutes now to review this chart. Then, when you're done with this chapter, review it again. Because it offers a comprehensive overview of savings and investing options, this may be one of the pages you go back to again and again.

Owning Property by Collecting

For a lot of kids, their first experience in investing is with collectibles. This is one of the easiest owner experiences for children.

 CFP TIP

Not all "collectibles" are really "collectibles." Make sure your children understand the value of their collection is only worth what someone is willing to pay for it. Avoid collecting fad items (toys tied to a new movie, for example) whose popularity may be gone in six months.

Here are some tips for helping your children have fun with collecting:

Start Small: Start with something your children like and would buy anyway. This can include things such as comic books, trading cards, action figures or toys.

Make it Educational: Collecting can be a great way to expand your children's horizons. Try collecting stamps to learn about the world, or coins to discover different currencies. Even baseball cards can help your children understand what traits separate a good player from a GREAT player.

Have Fun: Above all, have fun. If your kids' friends are collecting the same things, this can make for some fun trading sessions. While collecting can be serious business, it shouldn't become so serious that your children don't have a good time.

CFP TIP

If you collect things your children will want to play with (like toys), why not buy a couple extras? That way, your kids can start their own collection. Let them decide if they want to play with their collection or save it for later.

A PRICELESS COLLECTION? ONLY FOR ME.

When I was in my teens, I started collecting comic books. Every week, I'd go to the store and spend a couple of dollars on the latest superhero comics. I'd read it once and then carefully wrap it in a plastic sleeve for preservation. I probably spent about $400 in comic books and another $200 in protective sleeves. I heard about people who sold single comic books for hundreds of dollars and was certain that in a couple of years I'd get all my money back, and then some, when I sold my collection. I tried to sell it a couple of times and the most I was offered was $150 for all of them. When I went to college, the comic books got packed into boxes. It's now more than 30 years later. The comic books are still in the boxes. Occasionally, I'll unwrap one and read it. It brings back some great memories. Now, I don't want to sell them. At this point the memories these bring back are far more valuable than what anyone could afford to pay.

Sam, father of two

Collecting can be a great adventure. You can find treasures in all sorts of places.

Your Children and the Stock Market

With your help, your children may want to purchase part of a **publicly-owned corporation**. The ownership of a corporation is divided into "shares" of what is called common stock. Each share represents a fraction of the total ownership. The term "common" is by no means negative; all owners of a corporation are **common stockholders**.

Not every corporation is willing to share its ownership. Some companies are **privately held** and don't sell shares. The easiest way to distinguish between private and public companies is to look at the stock tables in the newspaper. Only those companies that are publicly-traded will be included in the stock tables.

If your children were to trade their dollars for common stocks, they would have the most to gain from a successful business and the most to lose from an unsatisfactory one. Common stocks in **successful companies** may come closer to offering all the advantages of an ideal investment than any other financial medium.

A good place to start understanding how common stocks work is the daily newspaper. Look for articles in the financial section and main news about public companies. Discuss the editorials and create a folder to hold clippings about the companies your children find interesting.

Investing in the stock market is not a sure thing.

 CFP TIP

You may need to be on your children's accounts as a "custodian," depending on their ages. As a custodian, you control all the transactions on your minor children's accounts.

STOCK PICKS

There are two options available if you and your children want to invest in common stocks. You can either blindly accept what others tell you, or you can take time to study and understand the essential facts that can affect you. Only when you understand the facts can you develop confidence in what you believe and why you believe it.

Let's be blunt, simply accepting what others tell you can be a foolish path to follow. You need to understand the facts regarding the characteristics, the short-term risks and the long-term opportunities of owning common stocks. **For some, buying common stocks can be like gambling.** If you don't know the facts, you have as much chance as succeeding in the stock market as you do in a casino.

Review the chart at the end of this chapter with your children and discuss how common stocks compare to other investments. Keep in mind, our chart is not all-inclusive. There are many factors you should consider before you invest. Making a smart investment decision requires an enormous amount of research and the resources to analyze the data. That's why so many people are now turning to professionals to help them manage their investments.

 CFP TIP

While watching TV or shopping, look for advertisements and products from the companies your children are interested in. This is an opportunity to turn TV time into learning time.

MONEY MATTERS

"The market has always bounced back from its lows and gone on to new highs. The greatest long-term financial risk you face is not stock market reactions, but in the continual loss in the value of a dollar."

James Stowers

THE DOW JONES INDUSTRIAL AVERAGE

To help your children understand the stock market's ups and downs, it might be helpful to introduce them to the Dow Jones Industrial Average (often referred to as **"the Dow"**). The Dow is the oldest and most widely quoted stock market gauge. Experts believe it represents the overall market at any moment in time. The Dow is made up of a selected group of 30 stocks. These stocks are chosen by the editors of *The Wall Street Journal.*

Sit down with your children and look at the graph. It shows the history of the Dow.

Here are some things to consider as you share this graph:

VALUE OF THE DOW ON THE 1ST DAY OF EACH QUARTER

QUARTERLY

- **Fluctuations** – The value of the Dow goes up and down like a roller coaster. Most of the changes are minimal, but occasionally (like in 2001) they are dramatic.

- **Long-Term Upward Trend** – The long-term trend of the Dow has been up since 1897.

- **Spurts (Uneven Trends)** – The upward trends are uneven. Many of the major moves are in spurts, few of which were predicted.

- **Always Rising to New Highs** – Since 1897, the Dow has always risen to new highs over time.

Information about the Dow can be found in the business sections of most major newspapers and on the Internet (look at cnnmoney.com or usatoday.com). Tracking the Dow can help give your children confidence in the potential of the stock market, as well as bring a continued understanding of how it operates.

Mutual Funds Offer a Diverse Investment

"I believe the soundest and safest place for me to invest my own money is in mutual funds that are searching for and investing in companies that are successful, with earnings and revenues that are growing at an accelerated rate."

James Stowers

Mutual fund investing allows your children to put their investment choices into the hands of professional managers. A mutual fund is a collection of stocks or stocks and bonds put together for a specific goal, such as growth or income. When your children, with your help naturally, buy mutual funds, they are actually purchasing small amounts of many different stocks and/or bonds. Compared to other investments, mutual funds offer many benefits. These include:

- **Professional Management** – Mutual fund managers are full-time professionals dedicated to managing the money invested in their funds. They bring with them a specialized team of researchers, analysts, and technological tools to make certain that the money invested, no matter what the amount, is given full-time attention. They invest, reinvest and seek the best opportunities for the money they manage.

- **Diversification** – Unlike buying shares of individual stocks, mutual funds spread investments over a number of different companies and sometimes, industries. Diversification is beneficial because some companies may lose value while others prosper. This means the losses of one company can be offset by the gains of another.

MONEY MATTERS

Estimates show that at least two million teens today are working with their parents as custodians to invest, both on-line and through traditional means.

What is the growth potential?

• **Opportunity for Growth** – While there is no guarantee, if the past is any indication, common stock mutual funds certainly offer an opportunity for growth, particularly over the long term.

• **Available in Convenient Amounts** – Many investment options require a large initial investment, which closes the door to small investors. Some mutual funds offer investment plans that allow investors to begin with a modest amount and add additional amounts on a regular basis.

• **Liquidity** – Depending on the strategy of the fund, you can withdraw part or all of your investment at any time. Some funds may require that you wait a period of time before you get your money to discourage you from "playing the market" and over-reacting to market fluctuations.

• **Current Information** – Information about your mutual fund investment is readily available. Simply call the mutual fund company or visit their Web site to track your account's progress.

HOW TO CHOOSE A FUND

There are literally thousands and thousands of different mutual funds. In theory, all mutual funds have access to the entire common stock and fixed income market, but not all are solid performers over time. How they differ depends on the combination of investment objectives, performance, ethics, qualifications of the managers, dedication and available support systems.

It is important that you and your children understand and believe in the investment philosophy, objectives and policies of any mutual fund in which you invest.

Answer the following questions:

- Is the philosophy logical? Does it make sense?
- How does the fund intend to implement its investment philosophy?
- Does it follow its discipline consistently year after year, or does it change its approach frequently?

Most importantly, examine the investment results of the fund.

- What is the record of the investment manager?
- Has the fund been successful over time?
- Are the results consistent?
- How do the results compare with those funds of similar objectives?

Of course, the fact that a fund, or any investment for that matter, performed well in the past does not necessarily mean it will in the future.

Where is the current management team heading and does this make sense to you?

 CFP TIP

Regular investing can enhance your potential for making a reasonable profit over time. When share prices vary, regular investments may reduce the average cost of a share and, therefore, your investments may ultimately outperform a one-time investment.

> *"I have never owned any marketable equity securities*
> *other than shares of mutual funds."*
>
> James Stowers

A BEGINNING INVESTOR

At the time of my nephew's 18th birthday, the subject of investing came up. As we talked, I realized that no adult had ever talked to me about this when I was a teenager.

Your investments can be a part of breakfast conversation.

We discussed investing in general and the value of compound interest over time. He was very interested and realized that his small savings account at a bank wasn't going anywhere. He asked a few good questions as we talked about stocks, mutual funds, CDs and interest earned in bank savings accounts. I suspected that this general conversation about investing was of some interest to my nephew, but that it would go nowhere unless we found a way to get him involved.

I saw an article in **Mutual Fund** *magazine on mutual funds that made a special effort to attract young investors. One fund had a low initial contribution, a newsletter designed to appeal to teens and an educational objective. The stocks held by this fund were companies that the younger investor might be familiar with.*

I offered to pay the initial $100. My nephew's job was to make monthly contributions of $50 on an on-going basis. Because he was a minor, his dad was to be the custodian.

That was in 1997. Today, my nephew has an account that he has faithfully invested into for a few years. He tells me he has learned quite a bit. It is only a beginning, but at least it's a beginning.

Phil, father of three

Buying and Selling

Although there's no way to predict when a mutual fund investment is going to be at a high or a low point, decisions to buy and sell must still be made.

Some of the factors you may want to consider before helping your children buy include:

- Do they have the required minimum investment amount?
- Does the selected investment meet their purpose? Can they tolerate the risk involved?
- Is there a convenient method available to buy (direct with a mutual fund company, discount broker, stockbroker or direct from a company)?

Some questions you might ask the investment company before helping your children sell their investment include:

- Will there be fees or fines involved if they sell?
- What sort of tax obligations will there be and who will pay them?
- If they're selling so they can have the money, can they earn the money they need through another source? (This will allow the investment to grow).
- What will they do with the money after they sell? Is there an investment with greater potential or that meets their objectives to a greater degree?

As your children are thinking about their decisions, it never hurts to remind them about the benefits that time (and the magic of compounding) will have on their investment. By investing early and for the long-term, their investment will have the best opportunity for growth.

MONEY MATTERS

When your children sell stocks or shares of a mutual fund for more than the purchase price, you (as the custodian) may be required to pay taxes on the profit.

ATTRIBUTES OF VARIOUS SAVING AND INVESTMENT OPTIONS

Use the table below to compare the attributes of various savings and investment options. This chart is divided into two categories – 1) Those savings or investment vehicles that children can do on their own, and 2) those that will require you to be on the account with them.

| | Activities kids can do on their own | | Activities that require a parent's name to be on the account | | | | | | | | |
| | | | LENDER INVESTMENTS | | | | OWNER INVESTMENTS | | | | |
	Piggy Bank	Collectibles	Savings Account	CDs	Money Market	Savings Bonds	Gold	A House	Individual Stocks	Stock Mutual Funds	Fixed Income Mutual Funds
Is there a minimum amount of money required to get started?	No	No	Maybe	Yes	Yes	Yes	Yes	Yes	Yes	Yes	Yes
Can your children get their initial money back?	Yes	Maybe	Yes	Yes	Yes	Yes	Maybe	Maybe	Maybe	Maybe	Maybe
Is their money easy to withdraw?	Yes	No	Yes	No	Yes	Yes	Maybe	Maybe	Yes	Yes	Yes
Is it burglar proof?	No	No	Yes	Yes	Yes	Yes	Maybe	No	Yes	Yes	Yes
Can their money grow faster than the shrinking value of a dollar? Short-Term*	No	Maybe	Maybe	Maybe	Maybe	Yes	Maybe	Maybe	Maybe	Maybe	Maybe
Long-Term*	No	Maybe	No	No	No	No	Yes+	Maybe	Yes+	Yes+	No
Can their money benefit from compounding?	No	No	Yes	No	Yes	No	No	No	No	Yes	Maybe
Is their money professionally managed?	No	No	Yes	Yes	Yes	Yes	No	No	No	Yes	Yes
Will they get regular progress reports?	No	No	Yes	Yes	Yes	No	No	No	Yes	Yes	Yes

* Short-term investments are less than five years. Long-term investments are those greater than five years.

+ Historically, these investments have grown faster than the shrinking value of a dollar. However, past performance is not an indication of future results.

This is for informational purposes only and is not intended as investment advice.

YOUR IDEAS AND EXPERIENCES

Abilities

Support the Family Business

Company Tracking

Pizza Fund Manager

THE INVESTING DECISION

Support the Family Business

When your children initiate a "business" i.e., lawn mowing, pet sitting, plant watering or house painting, they may need financial help to start it. By letting you invest in their business, they can get the funds needed and you can teach them how investments work.

At a family meeting, discuss the business, being sure your children mention any help, financial or otherwise, they could use from the family. In return for any help received, they can offer to pay a percentage of the profits each month for a predetermined amount of time. It should be understood that this is an investment, not a loan. If the business is not profitable, the money will not be repaid.

Siblings with savings or parents may invest cash to help get the business started. Those without money can still invest by offering to make or deliver flyers promoting the business.

For each investor, your children should make up a certificate (with a duplicate), similar to the one on this page.

The original should be given to the investor, and the business owner should keep the duplicate. Each month, the business owner should update the investors on how the business is progressing and pay them their percentage of the profits.

I agree to pay

_____
NAME OF FAMILY MEMBER

_____% of the profits of

_____
NAME OF BUSINESS

each month until

_____
DATE

in return for their investment of

$ _____

Signed,

_____
OWNER'S NAME

YOUR CHILDREN AND THE STOCK MARKET

Company Tracking

To help understand how large companies work and to become familiar with the daily newspaper, have each family member select one of the top Fortune companies (for example, Wal-Mart, Coca Cola, Pepsi, Disney, General Motors).

Using an envelope or folder, start clipping out articles that mention the companies you select.

Put a piece of graph paper on the outside and write the company name on it. Plot on the graph paper the daily price of the company's stock. Look for trends in the price of the stock. How does the news reported in the paper affect the price of the stock?

At the end of the month, have family members share what they learned about the company they are following. Track the company for a period of one year (or longer).

MUTUAL FUNDS OFFER A DIVERSE INVESTMENT

Pizza Fund Manager

Kids like to help add toppings to a pizza. Explaining a mutual fund to your little ones is easier when compared to a pizza.

What you will need:

- All of the makings for a pizza including several toppings

Tell your children to pretend that they are portfolio managers. Show them the pizza crust with sauce on it. Tell them that this will be the base for their fund. Next show them the topping ingredients. Tell them that these are like the stocks that they can choose from to make up their fund. Let them choose the toppings and place them on the crust. Bake the pizza. Cut the pizza. Tell your children that each person who buys a piece of the pizza is an investor and that piece is that person's share of the fund (or pizza).

- What would they call their fund?

- What is their fund made up of? (cheese, sausage, pepperoni, black olives, etc.)

- Is it easier for a person to buy a piece of pizza than to buy each item separately?

YOUR IDEAS AND EXPERIENCES

YOUR IDEAS AND EXPERIENCES

Smart Spending: Becoming a Wise Consumer

This chapter invites your children to understand

their power in the marketplace.

Part of being financially aware is learning how to be a wise consumer. This chapter invites your children to understand their power in the marketplace and to realize the kind of power the market has over them. You'll also share ways to make smart purchases and talk about:

- **UNDERSTANDING THE PURCHASE DECISION suggests questions your children can think about before they go shopping or make a purchase.**

- **COMPARISON SHOPPING explores ways to help your children find the best product and price.**

- **HOW AND WHEN TO NEGOTIATE provides your children with six pointers of negotiation to increase their shopping fun.**

- **KNOWING YOUR CONSUMER RIGHTS helps you guide your children through knowing when and how to complain.**

- **KEEPING AN EYE ON ON-LINE SHOPPING gives you guidelines to help make sure your children's on-line shopping experiences are safe and successful.**

- **RUNNING ON EMPTY. What do you want your role to be when your kids need more money?**

It's important to help your kids become wise consumers who think before spending.

Understanding the Purchase Decision

Sometimes we buy because we **need** something, other times we **want** something. It's important to fulfill needs. It's also important, and nurturing, to help your children fulfill some of their wants. The trick is to help your kids become smart consumers who think about how they are spending their money. Even when your children act spontaneously, they can feel in control of their purchasing decisions.

One way for you to help is to spend time talking with your children about their buying decisions. Use the time spent driving in your car together, or sharing a meal to bring up some questions they can think about before they go shopping or make a purchase. Some questions to think about include:

Help your children map out their shopping path.

- What are you shopping for?

- Do you *need* it? Do you *want* it?

- Do you absolutely *have* to buy it today?

- Do you have the money to make this purchase?

- Do you have the money to maintain your purchase (such as dry cleaning costs for certain clothing items)?

- What are you willing to give up if you spend your earnings or savings on this purchase?

- How many hours or jobs will you need to work to pay for your purchase? Is it worth it?

- Where do you find the best selection, price, quality and convenience for what you want or need?

- Will it be going on sale in the near future? Can you wait until then?

- Are you getting good value for your money?

- Are there alternatives to buying what you want or need, such as borrowing, renting, bartering, buying second hand or making it yourself?

- What if the store doesn't have what you want – what are your next steps?

With your help, your children will get in the habit of asking these questions before they buy. Understanding why they buy, and then being able to make well-informed purchase decisions, can help your children become smarter consumers.

CFP TIP

Watching television, with its numerous commercials geared toward children, can increase the amount of "wants" your children may have. Consider limiting the time your children watch TV, or add appropriate commercial-free videos to limit their exposure to commercials.

MONEY LESSONS FROM A PENGUIN

I was seven years old and my mom dropped my older brother and me off at the movie theater to watch a movie. We were about 20 minutes early so my brother and I went to the gift store, which was next to the theater. I had $8 in my pocket and thought it was a huge sum of money. After all, the movie cost $1. While in the gift store, I noticed a five-inch tall wooden penguin with glass eyes. It was truly a work of art and I sure wanted it.

My brother yelled over at me that it was time for us to get to the show so I walked over to the check out line and waited my turn. It was the first time that I remember ever standing in a check out line and buying something for myself. My brother was behind me so that at least gave me some comfort. The penguin did not have a price tag on it, so I had no idea what to pay for it. When it was my turn, I handed the cashier the penguin and she rang it up on the register. The total price came to $8.20. I could have died.

I reached in my pocket and took out my $8. I did not have enough money. I looked behind me in the line and there were four people waiting to check out. I was so nervous and scared. My brother gave me the additional twenty cents to cover the bill and I was able to check out.

What do you absolutely have to get today?

Between my brother and myself, we did not have enough money left over for both of us to see the movie. We decided that I would wait outside the theater and my brother would see the movie. By the time the movie was over and people were coming out, I had decided that the penguin was not worth the humiliation and embarrassment that I felt at the store, and it was definitely not worth missing the movie. All these years later, I still have that penguin.

Richard, high school teacher

Comparison Shopping

Once your children have made the decision to make a purchase, their impulse may be to run out and buy the first item they see. This urge can be costly if the first item they see doesn't offer the best price, quality or have all the features they want or need.

Discussing your method of comparison shopping will give your children ideas about how to carry out their own search and help them become financially aware consumers.

Your children can also research and compare their purchases through consumer reports in periodicals, books and on-line.

When comparison shopping, your children should keep the following things in mind:

Price – Some consumer items, because of their abundance and availability, are easy to compare while others are more challenging. Here are a few price-related questions:

- What is the cost of the item?

- Have you comparison-shopped and found the lowest price?

- Is the item worth its cost?

Some consumer items are easy to price compare and others are more challenging.

- Have you explored less expensive alternatives?
- Are coupons available for the item now or will there be in the future?
- Is there any resale value?

Influences – Purchase decisions can be influenced by many things besides your budget, including how you feel about certain issues such as the environment or supporting local retailers. Often times, it may mean you pay more for an item because of how an issue influences the way you feel. Here are a few questions to consider that can help you determine how an issue influences your spending decision:

Environmental Issues:
- Does this product represent my values regarding the environment?
- Am I willing to pay a premium for an environmentally friendly product?
- What if I bought a less expensive product that wasn't as environmentally friendly? How would that make me feel? Would I still enjoy it as much?

Supporting Local Retailers:
- Is the quality of this product higher than a comparable item at a large retail chain store?
- Am I willing to pay extra to support a local merchant?
- If I can get the same product at a lower price by shopping at a large retail chain, how would I feel about that decision? What if the product was of lesser quality?
- Am I willing to negotiate a lower price so I can still spend my money at the local merchant but get the benefit of the retail chain discounts?

MONEY MATTERS

*The Real Deal,
a booklet published by the
Federal Trade Commission,
features consumer
shopping tips for kids.
Call 1-800-769-7960
or refer to their
Internet site at
http://www.ftc.gov.*

Extras – Some purchases give you the opportunity to pay more to get extra features. These include service, support or shipping. For some people, these "extras" are as important as price and convenience. When considering these add-on charges, ask:

- What do I actually get by spending more?
- Do I really need these additional features?
- Can I get a discount if I decide I don't want one of the standard or additional features?
- Can I negotiate a better deal by having these included as part of the purchase?
- If service and support are offered, are they convenient to use?

Condition and Quality – Your children can research the quality of an item by reading about it, asking questions and comparing the item to others. Here are some questions you might ask them:

- What features does the item have?
  - Does it have all the features you need? Does it have some you don't?
    - Are you satisfied with the quality you see?
      - Have you talked to others who have purchased the same thing?
        - How long do you expect or need this item to last? Will the quality or condition of the item support this time frame?
      - Are you buying the best quality item that you can afford?
        - What is the return policy if you find you're dissatisfied with its quality or condition?

Are you paying extra for features you don't want?

Ease of Purchase/Convenience – The ideal purchase is easy and fun to buy. For some children, establishing a relationship with a storeowner or salesperson is an important part of purchasing. For others, convenience is more important. Your children may want to consider:

- How easy is the item to purchase?
- What is the return policy?
- How convenient is the location?
- How helpful and friendly is the sales staff?

Warranties – Merchants sometimes offer a warranty (a short-term, high-priced insurance policy that under certain conditions covers repairs or replacement) that often increases the item's price. When offered an extended warranty, teach your children to ask if their purchase already comes with a timed guarantee. A good rule of thumb is if your children can afford the cost of repair or replacement, they should not buy insurance.

 CFP TIP

If you live in an area where your children don't have many shopping options, on-line shopping and mail order catalogs can help them compare prices and selection.

DIFFERENT EXPERIENCE NEXT WEEK

My eleven-year-old daughter had been saving for months to buy a fancy bookcase for her bedroom. She finally got the money and we set off to the store she had researched. They had the best price and the best quality, plus free delivery and set-up. The clerk was on the phone when we arrived and waved that she would be with us soon. There were only a couple other customers in the store. We found the bookcase and waited. We waited more. My daughter went up to the clerk and asked for help. "All right," the clerk said and practically slammed down the phone. The clerk was sullen and my daughter surprised me by walking out of the store without buying.

"I want this to be fun," my daughter told me. "I want someone to be nice and pay attention to me."

I asked her if she wanted to report the clerk to the manager, but she didn't. Instead, we returned the next week at a different time, got a wonderful clerk who lavished attention on my daughter and she happily made her purchase.

Franklin, father of two

When it works, negotiating adds an exciting zing to your purchase.

"Often times, if you wait to buy something, you'll discover that the appeal is gone and you no longer have a desire to buy it."

James Stowers

How and When to Negotiate

The ideal outcome of a negotiation is a better deal (such as a lower price or free extras), and a more memorable relationship with the seller.

The types of businesses that welcome negotiations differ. Negotiations are expected at some businesses, such as flea markets. You and your children may also find some privately-owned businesses that offer small discounts or services to loyal customers and even some large franchises (such as department and discount stores) may also consider negotiating. **When in doubt, it never hurts to ask for a better deal.**

The type of business often indicates when negotiating may be possible, but you might suggest your children try negotiating when the product they're purchasing is less than perfect (such as stained or torn clothing), when it's a big ticket item (such as a car or stereo) or when they're buying in larger quantities.

CFP TIP

Some kids will be natural negotiators and others will hesitate or not want to negotiate. Watching you negotiate a purchase may give them ideas about developing their own style. Encourage them to find a negotiating style that feels comfortable.

Here are the six pointers for negotiating:

Power – Are you speaking to the right person – the person with the decision-making powers? If not, ask who might be able to help you.

Politeness – Be polite and respectful when you speak. Try using phrases like: "Would you be comfortable giving me a discount on this piece?" "Is this the best you can do on this item?" "I'm wondering if you could take any less on this item?"

Privacy – Speak in privacy so other customers don't inhibit your conversation.

Preparedness – Be prepared for a refusal or a counter-proposal. Consider what other deal would be acceptable. For instance, if your child is buying a new computer printer, maybe they could negotiate for a free ream of paper.

Partnership – Understand that the seller may not be able to give a discount or negotiate.

Pride – Tell your children, even if they don't achieve their negotiation goal that they should be proud of themselves for trying. When it works, negotiating can be a satisfying, confidence-building part of the purchasing process.

Before negotiating, be sure you are speaking to the right person, a person who has some decision-making powers.

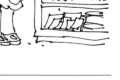

CFP TIP

Remind your children that in any purchasing situation they always have the power to walk away before buying anything. Even if they feel pressured or obligated, they are never required to complete a purchase.

Don't let a salesperson pressure you to buy something.

A LESSON IN LESS

"I want this painting and I am $5 short," my teenage son whispered to me. "Can you loan me $5?"

We were in an antique mall. The painting was $30, nicely framed.

"Why don't you see if you can negotiate and get a better price?" I suggested.

"What would I say?" he asked.

We rehearsed a few possible scenarios. He didn't really like any of my suggestions. He started to put the painting back, then suddenly walked over to the clerk.

"I love this painting but I don't have quite enough money," Andy said. "Can you take any less for this and still make enough money?"

The clerk stared for a moment. Then she took out a price book and looked up the painting.

"I can give you $4 off," she said.

"How about $5?" Andy asked.

She nodded.

My son's method seemed a little unorthodox to me, but it obviously worked very well for him.

Lucia, mother of one

Knowing Your Consumer Rights

What happens when the item purchased is not what your children thought it would be? What if something breaks or malfunctions? What happens when your children are ready to buy something, but the sales staff is treating them rudely or indifferently?

Part of being a wise consumer is knowing when and how to complain. When the product or service is not as promised or something goes wrong with it, it is natural to want to tell someone and have the situation resolved in a quick, easy and positive way.

When your children feel they have a reasonable complaint, consider:

- Creating a fact sheet – include dates, people and products or services.

- Having your child answer, "What went wrong and what do I want to happen next?"

- Deciding the best way to communicate the complaint.

Often a quick phone call can resolve the situation. Suggest they keep their fact sheet in front of them and be efficient and to the point. If they feel themselves getting angry, recommend they wait until they are calm to have the conversation.

If your children's phone call is not successful, they may register their complaint by letter. Some tips to consider when writing this letter include:

- Address the letter to the best person. It's often helpful to go "straight to the top" – such as the president, owner or manager of the business.

- Use a polite and rational tone.

- Using the fact sheet as a guide, clearly and thoroughly state the problem.

- Stay focused on the problem.

- Offer a solution or request an action.

- Give the letter reader a timeframe for taking action.

What happens when something breaks or malfunctions?

- End on a positive and firm note.
- Attach copies of any pertinent documents, such as sales receipts and warranties, and be sure to keep the originals of all documents.

MONEY MATTERS

Teach your children the importance of keeping receipts and warranty information. Put them in a place where they can easily be found.

Keeping an Eye on On-Line Shopping

These days, you don't have to leave home to go on a shopping spree – you just have to turn on the computer. On-line shopping can offer kids a chance to find unique items, to bargain hunt, to comparison shop and to become financially aware consumers.

Shopping on-line is easy, which can also mean that it's easier for your children (assuming they have a credit card or their own on-line account) to go beyond a budget and buy things they might not really need or want. Therefore, close supervision is recommended whenever your children are on-line. When they're ready to begin shopping on-line, here are some guidelines to think about:

- **The Engine that Could** – Explore some of the search engines that are designed specifically for comparison shopping. Simply type in "price comparison." Your children may compare the prices they find on-line with local prices.
- **Bargain Bytes** – Help your children look for on-line coupons before they buy. Type in "coupons" in your search engine.
- **Keeping Good Company** – Check out the company your children are interested in purchasing from and make sure it has a good reputation. Some companies have feedback areas, where you can hear from other customers. Some companies offer satisfaction guaranteed. Find out the return and cancellation policies. Make sure it's easy to find a contact e-mail or phone number on the Web site.
- **Tracking the Charge** – Make sure your children understand all the charges. What is the exact shipping and handling charge? Is insurance charged? Is there a re-stocking fee for returns?

- **Credit Comfort** – Always check the company's privacy and security policies to ensure that transactions will be safe. Some companies guarantee every transaction and promise their customers will pay nothing if unauthorized charges are made to a credit card.

With your supervision, shopping on-line can be a good training ground for your children to practice the comparison-shopping process. Just remind them that every on-line shopping trip does not have to result in a purchase. Sometimes researching products, and comparing features and prices can be all the satisfaction needed (just like window shopping).

Running on Empty

When your children come to you because they don't have enough money to fulfill a need or desire, it can help to have prepared your philosophy on the subject. Some parents don't mind lending money to their children for large purchases. Others believe their children should learn to live within their own budget while earning and saving for things they can't readily afford. Still other parents may use this situation as an opportunity for their children to learn about credit cards (while still under parental guidance).

The credit philosophy you develop should reflect your own personal money values and should be communicated to your children so they will know what to expect before a credit or loan situation arises.

These days,
you don't have
to leave home
to go on a
shopping spree.

YOUR IDEAS AND EXPERIENCES

YOUR IDEAS AND EXPERIENCES

SMART SPENDING: BECOMING A WISE CONSUMER

Abilities

New and Improved • **Off Season Shopping Extravaganza**
Phone Shopping • **Blind Taste Test** • **My Gift List**
Is Bigger Really Better? • **Research Project**
Neighborhood Swap Meet • **File It**

UNDERSTANDING THE PURCHASE DECISION

New and Improved

Television commercials are designed to appeal to you and your children. By having the following discussion with your children, you can help them become more aware of the methods used by marketers to influence them to buy their products.

Watch a TV program with your children. After the show, ask them what they remember about the commercials. Explain that the people who design and make commercials try to convince them that they need or should have their product in your home. Discuss the commercials with your children and see if they can spot the marketing ploys being used to prompt them to buy the product.

- Do they say it is "new and improved?"
- Are they using bright colors?
- Do the commercials use a catchy tune?
- Do they use words such as "sale," "special deal" or "act now?"
- Do they use kids in the commercials who exaggerate how much fun they are having?
- Do they use characters that kids are already familiar with such as music, sports or movie stars?
- Do they make you think you will be "popular" if you have the product?
- Do they offer you something for "free" if you buy it?
- Do they compare it to another product?

UNDERSTANDING THE PURCHASE DECISION

Off Season Shopping Extravaganza

As your children get older, and clothing needs and wants become more expensive, try to entice them with this fun idea for bargain shopping!

At the end of the season, when stores are bringing out their new lines, let your kids sort through the racks of clothes that have been marked down. If they will be growing and changing sizes before the next season, try to help them anticipate their next size and buy accordingly.

Bargain shopping can be tough because they will be choosing things that they will not necessarily get to wear right away. As you help them pack their clothes away, remind them of how much fun it will be when they unpack those clothes and find the bargain items right on top, ready to wear! (If a bargain really excites them, leave the price tag on so they can be reminded of what a great deal they got when they unpack the clothes).

COMPARISON SHOPPING

Phone Shopping

Your children are major consumers, so encourage them to shop wisely. Even though they may not be able to drive to several places on their own to comparison shop, they can still make some smart shopping choices by using the telephone.

If they have a particular item they are looking for, and feel comfortable describing it over the phone, have them do some preliminary shopping by calling several stores to compare prices. Don't forget to talk about customer service – and how important it is in the decision to buy something. Would you rather buy something from a person who is helpful and courteous or someone who is rude and unpleasant?

COMPARISON SHOPPING

Blind Taste Test

Sometimes products of one brand seem to have much more appeal to your kids than a comparable product of another brand. But, are they really better? Help them find out how products really compare by having them participate in a blind taste test.

1. Choose a product that your children have been particularly interested in. This type of test works especially well with cereals, cookies or sodas.

2. Purchase that product, a competitive brand and a generic brand.

3. Blindfold your children and have them sample each product.

4. Have your children rate the products in order of their liking.

Discuss the following questions with your children:

- Is the difference in taste worth the difference in price?

- Would you be willing to use the less expensive product if you got the difference in price added to your savings account?

- If products look and taste alike, why are they priced so differently?

COMPARISON SHOPPING

My Gift List

Children are often asked by grandparents for a list of things they want for birthdays or special holidays. The following idea will help your children learn about comparing prices. Grandma and Grandpa will also appreciate knowing where they can get the best deal!

When your children create their lists, have them look through various catalogs and visit local stores for the items they want. Beside each item, have them write the price and where the item can be found.

The following is an example of what the list could look like:

Item	Fun Book of Toys	Play Village	Toy Heaven	Toy Land
Green Slime Action Man	$9.95 - page 66	$10.50	$9.75	Don't Have
Monster Kit	$15.30 - page 59	Don't Have	$17.00	$16.50

COMPARISON SHOPPING

Is Bigger Really Better?

Sometimes you think you are getting a great value because a product comes in a larger box. Often, when you are buying cereal or chips there are three size choices. Is the biggest package the best value?

Take your children with you the next time you go to the grocery store. Show them how to comparison shop by reading the tag on the shelf and looking for the price per volume. Often the tag will tell you how much the item costs per ounce.

Take a calculator and let your children use it to compare prices for cereal to determine which size would be the better buy. The one with the lowest price per volume is the better value.

Find The Best Buy			
Item	Size	Price	Cost/Unit
Wheat Flakes	20 oz.	$3.16	$.16/oz.
Wheat Flakes	16 oz.	$2.75	$.17/oz.
Peanut Butter	3 lbs.	$4.21	$1.40/oz.
Peanut Butter	1 lb.	$2.63	$2.63/oz.

KNOWING YOUR CONSUMER RIGHTS

Research Project

Of course getting the best price is a big consideration when your children want to make a purchase, but knowing if the product is the best choice is a little more difficult to gauge.

Guides, such as *Consumer Reports*, are available in which products have been tested and compared. These, and others like them, can be purchased at your local bookstores, found on the Internet or at your library.

Next time your children want to make a major purchase (such as a bicycle, video game system, new computer or car) show them where to find *Consumer Reports*.

Have them look up their product and compare it to other brands being marketed.

How does it compare in:

- Price
- Features
- Reliability
- Durability
- Problems
- Resale Value

HOW AND WHEN TO NEGOTIATE

Neighborhood Swap Meet

Do your kids have tons of stuff, and yet complain that they have nothing to play with or do? Next time you hear the words "We have nothing to do" suggest that your kids set up a neighborhood swap meet in your driveway or front lawn.

Have your kids go through their items and choose things they no longer want and would be willing to trade. Invite several neighbor kids to do the same with their things. Designate an area for each kid to "spread his wares" and then have the kids take turns choosing items and making trades. No money need be exchanged!

A few tips:

- Ahead of time, set up a meeting with all the kids involved and their parents to establish the ground rules. Having everyone participate in setting the rules will make it more likely that everyone will follow the rules. A poster board with the rules written on it can serve as a great reminder throughout the Swap Meet.

- If your children are not willing to let their things go forever, they should not trade that particular toy or item. Chances are the things they put out for swapping will never be seen again.

- Kids might need some adult guidance to get started. For instance, when deciding, "Who gets to swap first?" you could pick playing cards. The highest card gets to swap first.

KNOWING YOUR CONSUMER RIGHTS

File It

Most adults have a system for keeping track of their important papers, such as bills, investments and bank statements. If your children's paperwork is included in your filing system, the filing cabinet can get overloaded pretty quickly. Help your kids create a filing drawer of their own.

Help your children set up a small filing cabinet, or give them one drawer of yours, in which they can keep their personal, school and financial documents.

You may have sections for:

- Health certificates and immunization records,

- Bank statements,

- Warranties/guarantees/receipts and Return Information,

- Financial plans/goals,

- Invitations, school papers and other keepsakes.

At least once a year, go through the documents with your children, throwing out those that are no longer valid or that are for products they no longer own.

YOUR IDEAS AND EXPERIENCES

YOUR IDEAS AND EXPERIENCES

Donations and Volunteering

Exploring Your Children's Giving Style

Finding Causes Your Children Like

Discovering Volunteer Opportunities

Using Family Funds for Giving

Giving to Family and Friends

Feeling Thankful

Notice what inspires your children's sharing and generosity.

Besides spending, saving and investing money, your children can also donate it to their favorite causes. Many times, this is the most rewarding option.

Kids love to feel like they are helping. Giving is exciting and energizing to children. This chapter discusses:

- **EXPLORING YOUR CHILDREN'S GIVING STYLE provides questions you can ask your children to discover what manner of giving inspires them.**

- **FINDING CAUSES YOUR CHILDREN LIKE suggests ways to research the charities your children may like for an experience that goes beyond reading annual reports.**

- **DISCOVERING VOLUNTEER OPPORTUNITIES can build your children's life skills and deepen their compassion. Here are hints for matching your children with volunteer opportunities.**

- **USING FAMILY FUNDS FOR GIVING can be a great way to teach your children about responsibility, setting priorities and charitable giving.**

- **GIVING TO FAMILY AND FRIENDS suggests opportunities to give in personal ways to those in need.**

- **FEELING THANKFUL shows how charitable giving and volunteering can help your children appreciate their own good fortune.**

Exploring Your Children's Giving Style

Your children may already be giving in many ways. To help them explore and expand their giving options, notice what inspires their sharing and generosity. See what sorts of situations and problems at their school, in the community or in the world interest or concern them.

> ## MONEY MATTERS
>
> *Financial donations made to organizations that qualify for 501(c)(3) status are tax deductible.*

Here are some questions your children can answer to learn more about themselves as givers:

- Why do I want to give?
- What do I like about giving?
- What kinds of causes do I feel strongly about?
- What kinds of charities do I want to know more about?
- What kinds of issues do I think need my support and help?
- Do I know anyone who's involved in those charities or issues?
- Can I give time, money or material goods?

Talk through these questions with your children to help them find a direction and manner in which they can give. Some parents find asking themselves these questions can heighten their own charitable passions.

Don't be discouraged if your child says, "But I only have $10! I don't want to give any of it away. I need it all!" Like sharing, giving may not be something your child naturally wants to do. However, the more you discuss and explore giving opportunities, the greater the chance your children will become interested in charities and issues that spark their generosity.

MONEY MATTERS

Talk about your own philosophy of giving. What does it mean to you? How has giving changed your life? How have people given to you?

 CFP TIP

To instill the habit, some parents require that 10% of their children's allowance be set aside for charitable giving. Other parents invite their children to decide what and how they will give.

Many people think that giving to charity requires writing a check. But it is not necessarily just about money. Giving can be just as valuable when you share goods, services and your time. For instance, some children choose to donate some of their own toys to other children in need. This type of donation can be just as meaningful to the recipient as a check, and just as valuable a lesson in giving for your children.

ONE PASSION INSPIRES ANOTHER

I had spent some time talking about charitable giving and volunteering with my twelve-year-old son, David, but I wasn't sure the conversation had really gone anywhere. He didn't seem too interested in any of the possibilities I brought up, so I dropped the idea. I continued my own giving, which at that point was just writing checks every month. Then David saw a program on TV about illiteracy and suddenly he wanted to do something. I was impressed that David, who was fairly self-absorbed, was interested in something outside his own world. I found a family-oriented volunteer program we could both be part of. Even though David wasn't usually that keen on being seen in public with me, he was eager to learn the skills so he could help other kids learn to read. Initially, I was motivated simply by David's enthusiasm, but soon, I got swept into the program. My own passion for giving got rekindled and David's work teaching others to read made him aware of his own blessings. The experience was rich for both of us and it deepened our relationship as well.
DeAnne, mother of two

Some children choose to donate some of their own toys to other children in need.

Finding Causes Your Children Like

Whether they're donating time or money, it's important that your children find causes that are meaningful to them. The more strongly they feel about something, the more likely they may be to give of their time and money. Your kids may already have a cause or charity in mind. If not, have them make a list of things that interest them. Your children may be drawn to:

Your kids may be drawn to helping homeless animals and pets.

- Preserving the environment and wildlife.
- Helping homeless animals and pets.
- Improving other children's reading skills.
- Sending less-advantaged kids to camp.
- Feeding the hungry.
- Helping behind the scenes with a theater or musical group.
- Working at an art fair.
- Walking for a health cause.
  - Helping other children in need, at home or abroad.
    - Supporting activities and organizations they enjoy, such as scouting, sports, music or the arts.

Once you and your children have made a list of causes, you can find organizations and associations that support them through the Yellow Pages, the Internet, news reports, stories in the media or by asking friends and family members.

RESEARCHING CHARITIES

After you've pinpointed charitable organizations that your children want to support, show them how to find out more about the organization before donating their time or money. The results of their research will help assure them that their donations are going to the best possible places.

To find out more, contact the organization and ask for their informational brochures or annual reports. If possible, talk to the executive director or development person at the organization, review their Web site, talk to other volunteers and donors or check with the Better Business Bureau. The Better Business Bureau's Web site (www.betterbusinessbureau.com or www.give.org) is a wonderful resource for tips on donating, as well as specific information on many charities.

With your research materials in hand, look for the following information:

- Who or what does the organization help? Is this the group, place or thing that your children would like to help?
- In what ways does the organization help?
- How long have they been around? Are they financially sound?
- What are their current goals?
- Where does money donated to the organization go? How much money goes directly for the cause (to the people, place or thing in need)? How much goes back to the administration and marketing of the organization?
- What kinds of volunteer opportunities do they offer? Are there age restrictions? Do they provide the necessary training and supervision?
- Are other children involved in volunteering or contributing?

MONEY MATTERS

The Web site of the Better Business Bureau Wise Giving Alliance (www.give.org) was formed through the merger of the National Charities Information Bureau and the Council of Better Business Bureaus' Foundation and its Philanthropic Advisory Service. The Alliance evaluates national charitable organizations according to 23 standards.

VISITING ORGANIZATIONS

If the organization your child is interested in is near you, visiting can be an ideal way to determine its suitability. Before you visit, call to set an appointment or to find a convenient time. Make sure your children are prepared with questions that will give them the information they'd like to learn.

Hopefully, your visit will give you firsthand experience about the people and causes it serves, its needs, staff and volunteers. Often, such a visit offers a powerful emotional experience that an annual report or promotional brochure cannot.

CALL TO CARING

My daughter and I went to visit a local organization that provides childcare for disadvantaged children. At age eleven, my daughter loves little kids and had read about this organization in the newspaper. We met the director, the woman who actually started the organization. She described the background of many of the children and told us how much they had been through, even though they were under five years old. My daughter was shocked and sympathetic. Then we visited the children. My daughter got to play with the two-year-olds and they seemed delighted with the extra attention. My daughter left impressed with the organization and its staff and feeling like she'd made a difference.

She began volunteering one day a week after school and also began donating small amounts of money. This volunteer connection has helped my daughter grow into a kinder, more compassionate person.

Patsy, mother of one

Before you visit the charity, make sure the organization is kid friendly.

OPENING UP BY GOING IN

Our family participated in a special visitation program sponsored by the Salvation Army. Our visits took us to different neighborhoods and introduced us to fascinating people. Our children learned other sides of life from meeting these people, and they learned how rewarding it was to give their time. As an extra bonus, my wife and I learned about the Salvation Army and were very impressed. We both began volunteering for them and had many wonderful hours helping.

Jill and Lee, parents of four

Discovering Volunteer Opportunities

If your children decide that volunteering their time is the best way for them to give of themselves, there are steps you can take to make their experience a rewarding one. Your children may already volunteer their time through church, school or various other programs. Like other types of work, volunteering can help your children develop skills such as:

- Working together with others.
- Listening.
- Following directions.
- Developing patience.
- Handling responsibility.
- Becoming more tolerant.
- Developing flexibility.

MONEY MATTERS

More than 55% of the United States' adult population spends 3.5 hours per week doing volunteer service.

Statistical abstract of the United States 2001

Before your children pursue volunteer opportunities, ask them the following questions:

- What kinds of help would you like to give? (If they don't know, that's fine. That's part of the discovery process).
- What kinds of people do you want to work with?
- What kinds of projects interest you?
- What are your time and transportation issues? What are the limitations on the number of hours you can spend volunteering?
- Do you want or need to work with family or friends? (Depending on the age and needs of your children, a parent or adult chaperone may need to accompany them during their volunteer activities. You may need to commit along with your children).
- Could this volunteer job be a springboard to a paying career in the future?

After discussing these issues, if you and your children are still in need of some volunteering ideas, consider exploring some of the following:

- Visiting seniors in retirement communities.
- Picking up trash in public parks and along highways. (There are even "adopt-a-highway" programs available in some areas across the country).
- Petting and walking abandoned pets at animal shelters.
- Helping during a charity's fundraising events.
- Reading books or playing games with children in hospital wards.
- Serving meals at homeless shelters.
- Organizing a food or clothing drive at their school.
- Beginning a letter writing campaign with the military overseas.
- Helping maintain a community garden.

MONEY MATTERS

Look for a City Cares organization in your area (www.citycares.org). These organizations help match volunteer resources with volunteer opportunities. If you're in a smaller town, call your local or regional United Way or Red Cross for volunteer ideas.

There are numerous ways your children can express their desire to give. Finding the way that will be most meaningful to your children may require discussion, research and also follow-up. Once they've spent time with their charity, make sure your children are getting the most out of their volunteer time. Ask them the following questions:

- Do you like the work the organization is doing?
- Do you feel welcomed and part of a group?
- Do you have something to do?
- Do you feel useful?
- Is there a different kind of work you'd rather be doing?
- Is your volunteer work keeping you from doing your schoolwork and extracurricular activities?

Find volunteering opportunities that make your children feel useful.

EARNING VOLUNTEER TIME

My teenage son, James, told me he wanted to go with a school group to Central America to work with Habitat for Humanity. "And it won't even cost that much to get there!" he enthused.

But the cost of getting there turned out to be more than I could afford. So I challenged James to earn his own transportation money and, to my surprise, he did. It was the first time he had earned money for something that wasn't just for him. The week he spent working with Habitat and helping others made a powerful impact on him. He learned new skills, made great friends and learned about working as a team. He also learned how lucky he is. The experience was life changing and opened my son up to giving and sharing in a dramatic way. Since then he has regularly given to charities and has volunteered at camps for disadvantaged children.

Dan, father of three

CFP TIP

Whether donating their time or money, make sure your children do not overextend themselves by giving too much. Help them find the amount of giving that is right for them and you.

MONEY MATTERS

Depending on the size of your family fund, consider consulting a financial advisor or your local community foundation for more information on setting up a fund or foundation.

Using Family Funds for Giving

For families who have the money and desire, **setting up a family fund or foundation can be a great way to teach your children about responsibility**, setting priorities and charitable giving. The amount of money in the fund isn't as important as giving your children the experience of discovering how and where those funds can be distributed. For example, one grandmother set up a fund and had her five grandchildren work as a team to figure out how to distribute the income each year. Another family of four gave each family member the opportunity to direct one fourth of the family's giving for each year. Each person had to research the organizations to which they wanted to donate and explain to the others why their gift was important and worthwhile.

TALKING ABOUT MONEY THROUGH GIVING

When my children were in elementary school, I set up a family fund as a way of demonstrating my value system and opening up money conversations with my children. We started talking about money through giving.

My goal was to make yearly contributions to causes the children liked. The fund was also a reminder for all of us that money can go for things outside everyday wants and needs. The fund inspired conversations about financial statements, which the foundation sent out annually.

The fund continues bringing up new financial topics. In a year when the stock market was not kind, the conversation turned to: Do we dip into principal and keep our same level of giving? Or do we cut back our contributions and maintain our principal?

I view this fund as a way to "groom my successors." Why wait until my children are in their 30s to talk about giving? I hope my actions and our conversations will help them discover their own ways to share resources.

Rusty, father of two

Giving to Family and Friends

Giving doesn't always have to be to charitable organizations and causes. Sometimes your children may want to give to people they know who are in need. The following are some families' experiences in giving to family and friends:

- One parent advised her children, "Give to the people who inspired and helped you this month or this year."

- Another parent gives part of her charitable donations to people who are going through especially hard times. After seeing her do this for years, her eleven-year-old daughter decided to give a special gift to a girl in her class whose parents were getting a divorce. "Sally seems too quiet and depressed. She hardly ever talks to anyone anymore," her daughter, Anna, explained. Anna did extra chores to earn money to buy Sally a lovely diary. That gift transformed Sally. She started coming over to the house and she and Anna became close friends.

Give a friend a special treat.

- One father sets an example by surprising hard working people at traditionally low-paying jobs with a little extra money. He'll give an extra $5 to a great waitress or $10 to a nurse's aide.

- Some families have a container where everyone drops their extra change. At the end of a couple months, the family decides together to whom they give the money.

In giving to someone close to them, your children may have the chance to see firsthand the joy their giving can bring to others. This joy, in turn, can prove to your children how rewarding the act of giving can be.

Discuss with your children the things they should be thankful for such as a stable home.

Feeling Thankful

Charitable giving and volunteering can be an ideal opportunity to discuss with your children the things in their own life that cause them to be thankful. Whether it is their own health, financial security, a clean environment or a stable home, your children may appreciate their own good fortune more while helping others. Use this opportunity to continue to talk with them about their charitable experiences, what they've seen and heard and how it all makes them feel. Consider comparing and contrasting the situations of those they helped with their own lives. Compliment them for sharing their time and good fortune with others.

YOUR IDEAS AND EXPERIENCES

DONATIONS AND VOLUNTEERING

Abilities

Spring Cleaning • **Wishing Well**

Birthday Gift • **Organize a Fundraiser**

Thermometer of Good Deeds • **Majority Rules**

Make a Coupon Book

EXPLORING YOUR CHILDREN'S GIVING STYLE

Spring Cleaning

When it comes time to clean out the closets, even very young children can take part in giving.

Explain to your kids that some children do not have toys to play with or nice clothes to wear. Ask them if they would like to help these children. If they do:

- When cleaning their rooms, have your children set aside the toys they no longer play with or the clothes that no longer fit. Try not to force them to give away things they are not ready to part with.

- Help them clean the toys or to make sure all "parts" are gathered neatly together. If boxes are broken, help your children repair them. Remind your children that even though you know the new kids will be happy to get whatever is given, they will feel even better if they get them as new looking as possible.

- Likewise help them make sure any clothes given are clean and folded neatly.

- This is also a good opportunity to throw away the things that are broken or have missing parts, and clothes that are torn or too worn to be shared. (Don't give broken toys, toys that are missing parts, or torn, dirty clothing to charities).

Let your children go with you to the charity drop off point, or let them help gather and put donations on your porch if the charity picks up from your home.

Be sure to tell your children how much the item's new owner will appreciate getting it and how nice it is for them to think about others.

EXPLORING YOUR CHILDREN'S GIVING STYLE

Wishing Well

There's something about public fountains … people love to throw coins into them and make a wish! Next to many fountains you will find a plaque naming the group that will get the coins.

Next time you pass a "charitable" fountain, tell your children about the charity that will get the coins. For example: "All of the pennies from here will help the sick children at the children's hospital." Let your children have a coin to throw into the fountain and ask them to make a wish for the charity. Example: "I wish this will help a sick child feel better."

FINDING CAUSES YOUR CHILDREN LIKE

Birthday Gift

Traditionally guests bring gifts to the birthday boy or girl. But what if your children have more things than they can use?

Talk to your children about how fortunate they are to have so many things. Then bring up the idea that instead of having guests bring a gift, asking them to donate an item to your children's cause. You may have to convince them that they will still have cake and ice cream, play games and have lots of fun. If they are agreeable and interested, let them pick a charity.

When sending out invitations, include instructions that rather than bringing a gift for the birthday child, a specific gift should be brought that will be donated to the charity of your child's choice. Some examples of requested items for gift donations are:

- Books – to be donated to the school library
- Toys – for Toys for Tots
- Canned Goods – for the local food pantry
- Mittens – for the clothes closet

At the party, be sure to display the "gifts" where all of the guests can see them. Talk about how nice they are and how happy they will make someone.

After the party, help your children feel pride in their generosity by taking them with you to deliver the presents.

FINDING CAUSES YOUR CHILDREN LIKE

Organize a Fundraiser

High school students are ready to take on the world. For many, a very rewarding first step is organizing a fundraiser for a worthy cause. Not only is it personally gratifying to see the results of their work, but they also learn great organizational and leadership skills.

If your children have a cause they would like to support, here are a few tips to get them started:

1. **Contact the organization.** Have your children ask specifics about how they can help. What kind of items does the organization need? How should they be packaged? Are there any restrictions?

2. **Outline a plan.** Include:

   - Name of the organization they are trying to help.
   - What activity they would like to do.
   - What they want to achieve.
   - When they would like to do it (time, date and place).
   - Any costs that might be involved.
   - How funds are to be raised to cover the costs.
   - Where items will be collected and stored.
   - How they will get the help they need.
   - Permission or permits needed.

3. **Find a sponsor.** Have your children visit with their school principal, counselor, minister or group leader to discuss their plan. Be sure they have all of their facts in writing and display a positive, motivated attitude.

4. **Get permission.** It is wise for your children to get everyone on their side including the charitable organization, group or school they are working with and the city.

5. **Enlist corporations to support the event.** The support provided could be monetary, but also might be goods or services, such as a trucking company offering to make deliveries, a storage facility offering to store collected items or a crafts store providing materials for posters.

6. **Recruit helpers.** Encourage your children to make posters to put up around their school, church or town. If their school has daily announcements over the intercom, your children can ask them to talk about their project. Tell them who they will be helping and make it sound caring, but still fun to do.

7. **Get publicity.** Your children should contact local newspapers, radio and television stations. The media often sets aside a certain amount of airtime for public service announcements. They can also ask their school's art club to make posters.

DISCOVERING VOLUNTEER OPPORTUNITIES

Thermometer of Good Deeds

Although volunteers give of themselves without expecting any rewards, recognition of their time and effort is very important.

Help your children create a thermometer of good deeds to keep track of the family's volunteer hours.

You will need:

- A large pressboard gift box
- Scissors • Glue • Markers
- Equal lengths of red and white ribbon

Have your children draw a large thermometer (approximately 12" long) on the pressboard box. Using the marker, have them draw the "hash" marks to represent each hour volunteered. Cut out the thermometer. Cut a small slit (the width of your ribbon) approximately 1 inch from each end of the thermometer. Glue one end of the red and white ribbons together. Insert the ribbon through the top and bottom slits on the thermometer, then glue the remaining ends together, making a loop that is tight, yet still loose enough to slide.

Start out with only the white ribbon exposed on the thermometer. For every hour a family member volunteers, slide the ribbon up so the red ribbon will indicate how many total hours have been volunteered.

USING FAMILY FUNDS FOR GIVING

Majority Rules

Most likely you receive numerous requests for charitable donations in your mailbox every week. Instead of simply deciding on your own whether to donate or not, let it become a family decision.

Before starting this activity, determine an amount to set aside in your family budget for charitable contributions.

Create a file for contribution requests. After several weeks hold a family meeting to discuss how to spend your family contribution budget. Go through your file with your children, talk about the organizations and what they are requesting. When reviewing the file, keep in mind the following:

- Have you received numerous requests from the same organization?
- Have you recently made a contribution to that organization?

- Do you know someone who might be helped by a particular charity?
- Look at how each organization spends its money. What percentage goes to the charity and what percentage goes to administration/fundraising?

Let all members of the family look over the requests and let each member discuss why they feel the family should support each organization or why not. After all requests have been discussed, let the family vote on which groups get a contribution.

GIVING TO FAMILY AND FRIENDS

Make a Coupon Book

Sometimes, the most thoughtful (and economical) gift that can be given is the gift of one's own time. Help your children create a coupon gift book for holidays or birthdays.

What you will need:

- Seven Index Cards for Each Child (five for gift coupons, one for front cover and one for back cover)
- Decorations (markers, stickers, pictures from magazines and glue stick)
- Staples

1. Have each of your children decorate two index cards (on the blank side) to be the front and back cover for their coupon books.

2. Write the following on the five remaining index cards:

To: *Kari*
From: *Lindsey*
I Promise to: *Make your bed*
Expires: *On your next birthday*

(The expiration date is to ensure that the children don't forget to fulfill their gift coupon promise).

Have your children think of gifts fitting the intended recipient's needs, interests or passions. For example, they can:

- Spend a morning playing quietly with siblings (so Mom can get things done).
- Take the dog for a walk (for a dog lover).
- Let someone borrow something of his or hers that the recipient has always admired (let your younger brother borrow your baseball glove).
- Rake the yard (to anyone with trees, particularly if they are unable to rake themselves).

3. Have your children fill in each of the five gift coupons to give as a thoughtful gift of their time.

4. Add the covers and staple on the left side, making a booklet.

5. Present or mail the book to the gift recipient.

YOUR IDEAS AND EXPERIENCES

YOUR IDEAS AND EXPERIENCES

Smart Learning: How to Keep Getting the Financial Information You Need

Putting Money in Perspective

Investing in Learning

Asking for Help: Finding Experts and Mentors

Letting Them Learn

Hold family money meetings.

A s a devoted CFP, you've given your children a great beginning for their financial future. This chapter invites you to give them some tools they can take with them wherever they go.

- **PUTTING MONEY IN PERSPECTIVE helps your children keep their money concerns in balance.**

- **INVESTING IN LEARNING discusses how your children can "pay themselves first."**

- **ASKING FOR HELP: FINDING EXPERTS AND MENTORS suggests how to locate financial role models that will add to your children's financial awareness.**

- **LETTING THEM LEARN discusses letting your children benefit from their own financial experiences (both the mistakes and the successes).**

Putting Money in Perspective

Money issues and concerns have a way of ballooning. At times, regardless of your values, money (or lack of it) can seem like the most important thing in life. In this consumer-driven world, you can help your children fine-tune their financial awareness by giving them chances to put money in perspective.

Some ways to help your children keep their money concerns in balance include:

- **Holding Family Money Meetings.** Regular family money meetings give everyone a chance to talk about both personal and family money issues. Use these meetings to catch up on budget matters, spending and saving choices, charitable contributions, allowance issues, financial challenges and successes.

Money issues and concerns have a way of ballooning.

Keeping these lines of communication open will give your children opportunities to share their feelings and ideas about money, while at the same time give you a chance to evaluate their financial progress.

- **Counting Your Blessings.** Taking the time to talk and think about what you and your children have, rather than worrying about what you may lack, can help take the emphasis off of money. When counting blessings with your children, remember to focus on some of the non-material things you may be grateful for, such as your family, your health, your friends and your talents.

Show your children all they have to be grateful for... including family, health, friends and talents.

THE COUNT REIGNS

When I first suggested we talk about our blessings, you should have seen the look on my daughter's faces. We were going through a period where they were very dissatisfied with the amount of their allowances and they were not in a position to readily earn extra money.

I began the count every Monday on the way to school. I started listing the things I was grateful for and included one personal thing about each daughter. For several Mondays, I was the only one who spoke. Then my youngest daughter said, "I'm grateful for finding matching red socks and only having to look for three minutes!"

We all fell apart laughing. Soon the older girls were chiming in. Now, it's a ritual that helps all of us get our week off to a great start.

Roseanne, mother of three

- **Discussing the Ups and Downs of Money.** Some parents cut out articles about people and money and discuss the way money affects others. These types of discussions can help your children think of ways they might react under similar situations, helping to prepare them for how they might deal with future financial events. This preparation can help build their confidence in dealing with financial matters.

Investing in Learning

You've probably heard the expression, "Pay yourself first." This phrase suggests that before you pay your bills and obligations you first set some money aside to invest for yourself and your future. The same idea can apply to your children's future. One of the greatest gifts you can give your children is the feeling that their talents and skills have financial worth. The best way to nurture these talents and skills is to invest their time and energy in their education and practical experiences.

The same is true with nurturing their financial skills. Working through this book with your children is a great first step. The following are some additional ways to obtain educational or practical financial knowledge and experience:

- **Learn More.** Find educational programs on finance and money geared toward children and their interests. Some youth organizations you might check into include:

Girl Scouts	Camp Fire Boys & Girls
Junior Achievement	YMCAs and YWCAs
4H Clubs	Your local community college
Boy Scouts of America	or sources for continuing education

- **Subscribe and Clip.** Subscribe to financially oriented magazines and clip articles about kids and money for your children to read. Staying financially informed reinforces the importance you place on money matters.

- **Make a Financial Scrapbook.** Keep a record of the financial journey by helping your children create their own financial scrapbooks. Suggest they include ideas, notes, receipts, bank statements, copies of stock certificates and stories about the first time they earned money. Include pictures, taken or drawn, of moments when they reached their financial goals.

Find youth organizations that include programs on money.

CFP TIP

Ask your children, "What are some ways you would like to invest in yourself? What would you like to learn more about? What financial skills do you have that you'd like to improve?"

Hands-on experience is often a valuable way to learn about money and finance.

Asking for Help: Finding Experts and Mentors

I would not be in business today if I hadn't been smart enough to ask for help.

I wanted to do it all alone, but I soon realized I was going to be burnt out before I made a living. I had to rely on other people too.

I read lots of books on money, but it was working for two important mentors that helped me understand what money is really all about.

Alexis, mother of two

A mentor is defined as "a wise and trusted counselor or teacher." Because hands-on experience is often a valuable way for your children to learn more about money and finance, an expert or mentor can be a helpful resource during your children's financial education. When looking for a suitable role model, being involved in the selection process will help ensure that you're as comfortable with the choice as your children are. During your search, here are some questions for your children to ask:

- Who seems to share your same or similar money values or who has values you admire?
- Who has a job that you admire?
- Who is the kind of adult you want to be like?
- What are your favorite locally owned businesses?
- Have you read or heard about anyone whose money expertise or

knowledge you'd like to know more about?

Your children's financial mentors do not have to be individuals you know on a personal basis. They can also be people you discover through the media and whose financial dealings your children track through news stories, Web sites or even correspondence. If you've helped your children select role models who will work with them, it helps to stay involved during the learning process. Your involvement can ensure the relationship is beneficial for everyone involved.

In selecting mentors, you may find that your children choose rock stars, sports figures and other famous people. These are popular and even admirable choices, but when researching these role models, help your children understand the less glamorous side of being famous. With fame comes a loss of privacy, the pressure to perform and be excellent at all times and the pressure to support themselves, their family and their staff of agents, managers and administrative help.

$ CFP TIP

Help your children connect with one of the people they admire. See if they can work with them for a day or interview them about their career.

A CIRCLE OF FRIENDS

When my son was a teenager, I put together a circle of friends to help him choose a career he would enjoy. We had meetings three or four times a year. Each person talked about what he or she did for a living and what they liked and disliked about it. The first circle was so interesting that my son's friends joined in at the second circle. My friends invited the kids to visit their place of work and talked to them about the skills and attitudes it took to enjoy and excel at their jobs. Those circles made a huge difference for my son. He saw his choices and he began learning more detail about areas of work that interested him.

Lloyd, father of one

Encourage your children to look for role models and mentors.

IT'S NOT MY BUSINESS

My daughter and I have very different money values. She likes to spend everything and I like to spend a little and invest and save a lot. We battled quietly over money, but finally, I got wise. I gave her an allowance. We agreed upon the things she would pay for, how much money she would earn and how much I would contribute.

From that rational starting point, things sometimes got grim. She instantly spent her money in ways that, to me, seemed frivolous. I bit my lip and muttered, "It's not my business." I didn't bail her out (well, I did, but only the first time). Once she spent all her school lunch money on an "amazing" sweater. She had to take sandwiches from home for lunch. Very humiliating it seemed, since "everyone" was buying lunch. I talked to her about choices and timing. Little-by-little she has gotten better. Our values are still different, but she's learning how to handle money in her own way. And I'm learning to let her.

George, father of two

Continue to reference this book as as your children get older.

Letting Them Learn

By sharing the information you've taken from this book and enjoying the Ability activities, you should be well on your way to raising financially aware children. When age appropriate, give everything a try, take notes of what worked well and why. Use this book as a reference tool as your children get older, with subsequent children, or even with the next generation of children.

Remember, the most important and rewarding learning experiences you can give your children come when you:

- **Communicate** – Talk to your children when you shop, work, pay bills, make financial decisions or charitable donations. Tell them what you are doing and why. They will be listening, absorbing and appreciating the fact that you've included them.

- **Start Early** – Young children may not be able to count money, but they can understand trading, sharing and giving. As they grow, each early lesson and activity that you share with them will make it that much easier for them to reach financial awareness.

- **Stay Involved** – It is usually easier trying new things (such as making your first purchase, opening your first checking account or negotiating a purchase) knowing there's someone knowledgeable close by to give you advice. To help your children's financial confidence grow throughout their lives, keep asking questions and providing a hand when needed.

- **Let Them Experience Things Firsthand** – There's no better teacher than experience. As many of the Ability activities suggest, you can start by simulating experiences at home, but ultimately, take your children into the "real world" and, with your supervision, let them try things themselves. There's not much that makes children prouder than the first time they pay for their own snack or toy!

Finally, remember, your children are going to make mistakes. They're going to spend their money in ways that you find foolish and frivolous. This is all part of the learning process. Applaud their creativity and spontaneity. Help them solve problems – when they ask. You've given them a great start, now watch them take off. Your children may wander off course a bit, falter, almost run out of gas, but with your help, they should ultimately soar!

...they're going to make mistakes and spend their money foolishly...

YOUR IDEAS AND EXPERIENCES

YOUR IDEAS AND EXPERIENCES

SMART LEARNING: HOW TO KEEP GETTING THE FINANCIAL INFORMATION YOU NEED

Abilities

The "Great Eight" Value Adventure

Thanks in a Capsule

That's the Way the Money Goes • When I Grow Up...

Scrapbook

PUTTING MONEY IN PERSPECTIVE

The "Great Eight" Value Adventure

To build a family, you need a lot of tools. Money is just one of them. What role does money play in your financial dreams? Is it the fuel? The springboard? The end result? Knowing where money fits into your value system helps you focus and be more aware of your money actions and conversations.

Make your Great Eight list of eight things **you** most value in life in the order of their importance. Where does money rank on your list? How much time and energy do you spend on it in your daily life?

Your Great Eight

1. _____
2. _____
3. _____
4. _____
5. _____
6. _____
7. _____
8. _____

What did you learn from the Great Eight exercise about you and money? Are you living your life in a balance of work, money, family, fun and spirituality that feels good to you? Are you too focused on money or not focused enough? Do you feel comfortable having lots of money? Do you feel guilty when you have lots of money? Do your children have permission to be wealthy or do they have negative stereotypes about the rich?

These are great questions to discuss with your children.

Now, create a Great Eight list with **your family.** This exercise helps you clarify your own values and learn what your children value. This exercise also lets your kids know they are an important part of creating a family values picture.

Your Family's Great Eight

1. _____
2. _____
3. _____
4. _____
5. _____
6. _____
7. _____
8. _____

Here are some ways you can get financial conversations started:

- Tell a story from your own life when you realized there were things more important than money.

- Ask your children what they feel are the most important things in their lives. You may need to start by telling them the most important things in your life.

- Show your family your Great Eight list. Ask them to tell you what they would add and where they agree and disagree.

$ CFP TIP

Save your lists. Do this as a regular activity, so you can see how values change and evolve.

YOUR IDEAS AND EXPERIENCES

PUTTING MONEY IN PERSPECTIVE

Thanks in a Capsule

A time capsule makes a fun tradition on Thanksgiving as each jar is opened to remind us of things that we may have forgotten we were once thankful for.

For each family member you will need:

- An old shoebox, empty coffee can or pickle jar to act as the time capsule

- Scrap paper

- Pen

- A safe place to store the capsule

Have each family member mark their capsule with their name. Capsules may be decorated as desired.

On Thanksgiving have each family member write something they are currently thankful for on a sheet of scrap paper, date it and place it in their time capsule. Place the time capsules in a safe spot where they can be easily found next year.

Every Thanksgiving, allow each family member to open their time capsule to remind them of what they had previously been thankful for. If they wish to share what was on their paper with other family members they can. After reading, have them again write what they are thankful for this year, date it and add it to their capsule.

Continue the tradition throughout life.

PUTTING MONEY IN PERSPECTIVE

That's the Way the Money Goes

Create a chart similar to the one shown below to fill in at family money meetings showing exactly where the family's money was spent.

	Jan	Feb	Mar	Apr	May	Jun	Jul	Aug	Sep	Oct	Nov	Dec	TOTAL
Income													
Mortgage/Rent													
Natural Gas													
Electricity													
Water													
Car													
Gasoline													
Trash													
Groceries													
Insurance													
Clothes													
Savings													
Donations													
Telephone													
Internet													
Cable TV													
Entertainment													
Other													
TOTAL													
Difference													

Discuss the following: • What is the most expensive category? • Did the family get full value for the money spent?

INVESTING IN LEARNING

When I Grow Up...

Kids of all ages like to imagine what they will be when they "grow up." Spend some time helping your kids dream…and dream along with them yourself.

Initiate a discussion with your children about what they would like to be when they grow up.

Ask:

- What they think the job requirements are for their chosen profession…doctor, chef or electrician?

- What kind of education will they need … medical school, cooking school, electrical training?

- Where can they get the right education for their profession … college, vocational/technical school or apprenticeships?

- How much will it cost to get that education? Where will they get the money to pay for it?

- What kind of classes can they take in school now to help prepare for their career?

- How much money will they make?

For younger kids, the idea is simply to make them start thinking about their future. For older kids you can help guide them to the library or the Internet to research their dream professions and find sources for the education necessary to become what they want. Help them choose the best courses in high school to lead them to their dreams.

LETTING THEM LEARN

Scrapbook

Children's scrapbooks are often full of pictures of important events in their lives. When compiling their scrapbooks, encourage your children to keep mementos of their financial history as well. They will want to include:

- Things they wanted.
- Things they saved for.
- Things they bought.
- Donations they made.
- Their first pay stubs.
- Their first bank statements.

Make a scrapbook for your children that tracks their successes – including financial.

YOUR IDEAS AND EXPERIENCES

YOUR IDEAS AND EXPERIENCES

Additional Resources

SUGGESTED READING:

Bamford, J. (2000). *Street Wise: A Guide for Teen Investors.* Princeton, NJ. Bloomberg Press.

Barbanel, L. (1994). *Piggy Bank to Credit Card: Teach Your Child the Financial Facts of Life.* New York City. Three Rivers Press.

Benson, P.; Galbbraith, J.; Esplend, P. (1998). *What Kids Need to Succeed: Proven, Practical Ways to Raise Good Children.* Minneapolis, MN. Free Spirit Publishing.

Bernstein, D. (1992). *Better Than a Lemonade Stand: Small Business Ideas for Kids.* Hillsboro, OR. Beyond Words Publishing.

Beroff, A.; Adams, T.R. (2000). *How to be a Teenage Millionaire.* Irvine, CA. Entreprenuer Press.

Blue, R.; Blue, J. (1992). *Raising Money Smart Kids: How to Teach Your Children the Secrets of Earning, Saving, Investing and Spending Wisely.* Nashville, TN. Thomas Nelson Publishing.

Bodnar, J. (1999). *Kiplinger's Dollars & Sense for Kids: What They Need to Know About Money - and How To Tell Them.* Washington, D.C. Kiplinger Books.

Bodnar, J. (1993). *Kiplinger's Money-Smart Kids (and Parents, Too!)* Washington, D.C. Kiplinger Books.

Briles, J. (2000). *Smart-Money Moves for Kids: The Complete Parent's Guide.* Aurora, CO. Mile High Press.

Cipani, E. (1999). *Helping Parents Help Their Kids: A Clinical Guide to Six Child Problem Behaviors.* New York City. Brunner/Mazel.

Dobrin, A. (2001). *Teaching Right from Wrong: 40 Things You Can Do to Raise a Moral Child.* New York City. The Berkley Publishing Group.

Drew, B. (1992). *Money Skills.* Hawthorn, NJ. Career Press.

Drobot, E. (1987). *Amazing Investigations: Money. Find Out the Facts. Making Money, Spending Money, Money Stories and Much More!* New York City. Prentice Hall.

Duguay, D. (2001). *Send Money! A Financial Survival Guide for Young Adults on Their Own.* Naperville, IL. Sourcebooks Inc.

Estess, P.; Barocas, I. (1994). *Kids, Money & Values: Creative Ways to Teach Your Kids About Money.* Cincinnati, OH. Betterway Books.

Friel, J.; Friel, L. (2000). *The 7 Best Things (Smart) Teens Do.* Deerfield Beach, FL. Health Communications, Inc.

Godfrey, N.; Edwards, C. (1994). *Money Doesn't Grow on Trees: A Parent's Guide to Raising Financially Responsible Children.* New York City. Simon & Schuster.

Godfrey, N.; Richards, T. (1996). *A Penny Saved: Teaching Your Children the Values and Life Skills They Will Need To Live In the Real World.* New York City. Simon & Schuster.

Houser, P.; Bradley, H. (1997). *How to Teach Children About Money: A Step-By-Step Guide to Help Children Learn About Earning, Saving, Spending and Investing Their Money.* Denver, CO. Western Freelance Writing Service, Inc.

Hunt, M. (1998). *Debt Proof Your Kids.* Nashville, TN. Broadman and Holman.

Johnson, S.; Carson, J. (2000). *Grandloving: Making Memories with Your Grandchildren.* Fairport, NY. Heartstrings Press.

Jones, V. (1987). *Kids Can Make Money Too! How Young People Can Succeed Financially. Over 200 Ways to Earn Money and How to Make It Grow.* Salt Lake City, UT. Publishers Press.

Karlitz, G.; Honig, D. (1999). *Growing Money: A Complete Investing Guide for Kids.* New York City. Price Stern Sloan.

Kiyosaki, R.; Lechter, S. (2000). *Rich Dad Poor Dad: What the Rich Teach Their Kids About Money - That the Poor and Middle Class Do Not!* New York City. Warner Books.

Kiyosaki, R.; Lechter, S. (2001). *Rich Kid Smart Kid: Giving Your Child a Financial Head Start.* New York City. Warner Books.

Kourilsky, M. (1983). *Mini Society: Experiencing Real-World Economics in the Elementary Classroom.* Menlo Park, CA. Addison Wesley Publishing Company.

Lewin, E.; Ryan, B. (1994). *Simple Ways to Help Your Kids Become Dollar-Smart.* New York City. Walker and Company.

Mackall, D. (1994). *Kids Are Still Saying the Darnedest Things.* Rocklin, CA. Prima Publishing.

McCurrach, D. (2000). *The Allowance Workbook For Kids and Their Parents.* Franklin, TN. Vaughan Printing Inc.

McCurrach, D. (2000). *Kids' Allowances: How Much, How Often, and How Come.* Franklin, TN. Vaughan Printing Inc.

McNeal, J. (1992). *Kids as Customers: A Handbook of Marketing to Children.* New York City. Lexington Press.

Pearl, J. (1999). *Kids and Money: Giving Them the Savvy to Succeed Financially.* Princeton, NJ. Bloomberg Press.

Rosemond, J. (1981). *Parent Power! A Common-Sense Approach to Parenting in the 90's and Beyond.* Kansas City, MO. Andrews and McMeel.

Shelly, S. (2001). *The Complete Idiot's Guide to Money for Teens: Straight Talk on Making, Saving, and Spending Your Own Money. Great Advice on How to Manage Your Money Yourself.* Indianapolis, IN. Alpha Books.

Stahl, M. (2000). *Early to Ri$e: A Young Adult's Guide to Investing ... and Financial Decisions That Can Shape Your Life.* Los Angeles, CA. Silver Lake Publishing.

Stawalski, W. (2000). *Kids, Parents & Money: Teaching Personal Finance from Piggy Bank to Prom.* New York City. John Wiley and Sons, Inc.

Stowers, James E. (2000). *Yes, You Can...Achieve Financial Independence.* Kansas City, MO. Stowers Innovations, Inc.

Taylor, B. (2001). *More Fun Less Stuff: Starter Kit.* Takoma Park, MD. Center for a New American Dream.

Whitcomb, J. (2000). *Capitate Your Kids: Teaching Your Teens Financial Independence. They Do the Work, You Save the Money.* Milwaukee, WI. Popcorn Press.

WEB SITES:

BuckInvestor.com: www.buckinvestor.com

Choose to Save: www.choosetosave.org

Consolidated U.S. Govt. Web Resources: www.mymoney.gov

Consumer Jungle: www.consumerjungle.org

Cyberchase: www.pbskids.org/cyberchase

Escape from Knab: www.escapefromknab.com

Family Fool: www.fool.com/familyfool

Investing for Kids: www.thinkquest.org

It All Adds Up: www.italladdsup.org

Jump Start: www.jumpstart.org

Kids' Money: www.kidsmoney.org

Learning Bank: www.fdic.gov/about/learn/learning

Lifesmarts: www.lifesmarts.org

Savings Bonds: www.savingsbonds.gov

Smart Start: www.cibc.com/smartstart

Teens & Investing: Young Fools: www.fool.com/teens/teens.htm

Wise Pockets: www.umsl.edu/~wpockets

Yes, You Can: YesYouCanOnline.info

Young Money: www.youngmoney.com

Youth and Investing: www.better-investing.org

GLOSSARY:

Words and terms used throughout this book have been defined here with simple explanations. More detailed definitions may be found in financial dictionaries, as well as at YesYouCanOnline.info.

account – term used to describe money held by a bank or an investment company for the depositor.

allowance – a planned sum of money (either given on a regular basis or for chores done) that helps children learn money management.

annual report – a yearly record of an organization's financial condition distributed to shareholders. Included in the report is a description of the organization's operations, balance sheet and income statement.

appreciation – an increase in the value of an asset (such as a stock, bond, mutual fund or real estate) over time.

asset – anything that can be sold or has an exchange value. This includes savings, property, stocks and collectibles.

ATM (Automated Teller Machine) – a machine at which people can perform banking transactions, such as withdrawing, transferring or depositing money from their accounts.

barter – to trade articles and services without using money.

bond – a security that obligates the issuer to pay the bondholder a specified sum of money, usually at specific intervals, and to repay the principal amount of the loan at maturity. Bondholders have an IOU from the issuer, but no corporate ownership privileges, as stockholders do.

budget – a financial plan in which income and expenses are estimated and compared for a specified time period.

capital gains – the positive difference between the purchase price and the selling price of an asset; a profit from the sale of investments or property.

certificate of deposit (CD) – a type of federally-insured savings account in which a depositor agrees to lend their money to a bank for a predetermined amount of time. Cash withdrawn prior to the maturity date may incur a substantial penalty.

check – a written order to a financial institution to pay a specified amount of money to a particular person or company from money in the depositor's account.

checkbook balancing – the act of comparing the numbers in your checkbook against those on your bank statement to make certain neither you or the bank has made an error.

common stock – units or shares of a public corporation which are available to be purchased by the public. Purchasing shares of common stock is considered an owner investment.

compounding – when your money earns interest, not only on the principal, but also on any interest that was earned earlier. For example, if you have $100 growing at 10% per year, it will be $110 in one year (having increased by $10), and then $121 in the second year (having increased by $11), and $133 in the third year (having increased by $12).

consumer – a person who trades their money for goods and services.

coupons – certificates offering discounts on goods or services.

credit card – a plastic card issued by a bank, retail store or other creditor giving consumers the right to purchase goods or services and pay for them later. Most credit cards offer a grace period during which interest is not charged. After that, consumers are charged interest on the balance until it is paid off.

currency – any kind of money that is used as a form of exchange.

custodian – the person (usually a parent) who is responsible for a minor child's savings or investment account.

deposit – cash, checks or securities given to a bank or other institution for credit to the customer's account.

discount broker – a stockbroker who buys or sells your stock or bond orders but, unlike a "full-service broker," does not give you advice on your investments.

diversification – buying securities of different investment types, industry types, risk levels and companies in order to reduce your level of risk (or loss) if something should damage the business of any one of your investment holdings.

dividends – money a shareholder receives from a company as a result of the company earning a profit.

Dow Jones Industrial Average (the Dow) – an indicator showing generally how the stock market is going. The Dow is an average of the prices of 30 stocks which represent a wide array of industry types.

electronic transactions – financial dealings that are made through the use of computers.

expenses – the amount paid for goods and services.

Federal Deposit Insurance Corporation (FDIC) – this federal agency insures (within limits) your funds on deposit in member institutions. Banks and institutions pay the FDIC to insure individual deposits and protect their customers from possible loss.

Federal Reserve – a system of 12 regional reserve banks. Each Federal Reserve bank monitors the commercial and savings banks in its region to make certain they follow industry regulations. The reserve banks act as depositories for member banks in their regions, providing money transfers and other services.

fixed income – an investment that pays a predetermined rate of return, such as a bond, CD or savings account.

gross pay – total amount of a salary before taxes, insurance, benefits and other expenses are taken out.

income – money earned from work, investments and the sale of goods or services.

interest – the cost for the use of borrowed money paid by the borrower. For example, you receive interest when you allow a bank to use your money. You pay interest when you borrow money from a bank.

investment – using money, time or energy to create more money or reach a goal. Investments can either be financial (where money is invested to reach a financial goal) or can be an investment of time, talent and effort on the part of an individual (such as an investment in a college education to achieve future career success).

lender investment – an investment in which a bank or financial institution borrows your money in exchange for a set sum of money (interest). At the end of the loan period, the full amount you lent is returned to you. Examples of lender investments include savings accounts, CDs and money market accounts.

liability – debts or financial commitments.

liquidity – the ability to convert your assets into cash. The easier it is to get cash from an investment the more "liquid" the investment.

loan – a transaction in which an amount of money is borrowed for a specified period of time with the agreement that the money will be paid back to the lender within a certain time period. The loan often involves interest paid to the lender by the borrower.

mentor – a wise and trusted counselor or teacher.

money market – an account which invests in short-term investments (such as CDs and treasury bills) and offers checkwriting abilities. Typically, money market accounts require a minimum deposit and limit the number of checks that can be written over a given time period. Funds are available to depositors at any time without penalty.

mutual fund – a professionally managed investment portfolio that offers individuals the ability to invest in a collection of stocks or stocks and bonds put together for a specific goal, such as growth, income or capital preservation.

negotiation – the act of talking to others with the hope of gaining a more favorable deal on a purchased item.

net pay – the amount of salary received after taxes, insurance, benefits and other expenses have been taken out.

owner investment – an investment in which you become part (or full) owner of a business or property, thereby sharing in some of the risks and rewards of ownership. Examples of owner investments include mutual funds, common stocks, real estate and collectibles.

profit – a positive difference between the purchase price and selling price. If the selling price is higher than the purchase price, there is a profit.

resource – individual assets (such as money, property, other people, talent or skill) that can be used to support or help you reach a goal.

return – used to describe the money made (or lost) on an investment.

risk – the probability that an original investment might drop in value; the chance of non-payment of a debt.

savings – money that is held or collected for future use.

share – a single unit of ownership in a corporation or mutual fund.

shareholder – a person who owns stock (or shares) in a company.

stockbroker – a person who facilitates the buying and selling of securities, such as stocks or bonds. As payment for services, commission is collected based upon a percentage of the value of the transaction or assets.

Y ou are the ideal teacher for your children. However, are you prepared to teach them the life skills they need to get on the path to financial independence? Consider these questions:

- Do you want your children's quality of life to be as good as or better than yours?
- Do you want your children to make sound financial decisions?
- Do you need help in guiding your children in the process of becoming financially aware?
- Would you like to take a more active role in teaching financial literacy?

If you answered "yes" to one or more of these questions, then you'll find the information at **YesYouCanOnline.info** to be a valuable resource. The lessons and resources here help you teach kids to appreciate the value of a dollar, choose work they like, earn a good living and the importance of investing for the long-term. There's even a free curriculum that teachers can use to bring these valuable lessons into the classroom.

"If you don't talk to your kids about money, who will?"

James E. Stowers,
Founder, American Century Investments

Start using the resources at **YesYouCanOnline.info** today. While you're there – sign up for our FREE weekly emails and quarterly **Yes, You Can** publication.

YES YOU CAN

Visit **YesYouCanOnline.info** today and learn how to improve your financial position and help your kids get on the path to financial independence.

Dear Reader:

While reading and using this book, we encourage you to contact us with your experiences, suggestions and comments so we may further help parents raise financially aware children. Please contact:

Yes, You Can…
4500 Main
Kansas City, MO 64111
E-mail: info@YesYouCanOnline.info